The Long Emancipation

The Nathan I. Huggins Lectures

IRA BERLIN

The Long Emancipation

The Demise of Slavery
in the United States

HARVARD UNIVERSITY PRESS

Cambridge, Massachusetts,
and London, England

2015

FIRST PRINTING

Library of Congress Cataloging-in-Publication Data
is available from the Library of Congress

ISBN 978-0-674-28608-5

Contents

The Long Emancipation

Introduction

Hɪsᴛᴏʀʏ ɪs ɴᴏᴛ about the past; it is about arguments we have about the past. And because it is about arguments that we have, it is about us. In the study of American history, few arguments have been as impassioned and persistent as the seemingly endless debates about the nature and causes of slavery's demise. Who did it, how, and why—and ultimately, what was its meaning? The tenacious nature of this argument speaks to the centrality of freedom in American life, which, in turn, is embedded in the very meaning of American citizenship as stated in the nation's founding charters and in its connection to the nation's most critical contemporary social problem: racism. For the American people, the struggle to abolish slavery, secured by constitutional amendment almost 150 years ago, remains very much alive among us and about us.

The Long Emancipation enters that debate, being the story of the transformation of millions of men and women from property to person. It thus speaks to both the historic moment of the American republic's birth and the subsequent struggle to meet its founding ideal. In the twentieth and twenty-first centuries, as in the eighteenth and nineteenth, the question of freedom has remained inescapably political—tightly linked to the character and the aspirations of the American people and their polity—whether in its most accessible forms of popular culture or in the densest academic studies.

From these distant edges of historical understandings, *The Long Emancipation* redirects the ongoing argument respecting slavery's end and its implications. The argument itself can be found at almost every moment the question of slavery's demise comes to the fore.

For example, in the late summer of 1865, Major Martin Delany, the highest-ranking black officer in the Union army, whose imposing title did little to conceal a long, well-known record of abolitionist radicalism, stood before an audience of liberated slaves totaling some 500 to 600 men and women near the Brick Church on St. Helena Island, in South Carolina's lowcountry. Delany, according to an eyewitness named Edward Stoeber, a white officer who had been tasked with following him, "made them acquainted with the fact that slavery is absolutely abolished, throwing thunders of damnations and maledictions on all the former Slaveowners and People of the South, and almost condemning their souls to hell." Most importantly, he wanted the assemblage "to understand that we would not have become free, had we not armed ourselves and fought out our independence."[1]

Delany had hardly finished his outburst, when Stoeber grasped the import of this representation of the arrival of freedom and took issue with it. The slaves, he believed, had not secured freedom through their own struggle; rather, "our President Abraham Lincoln declared the Colored race free," he said, adding that Delany's outburst was "decidedly calculated to create bad feelings against the Government."[2]

The verbal kerfuffle on St. Helena Island in the aftermath of the Civil War was neither the first nor the last confrontation between those who believed emancipation had been achieved by the hand of ordinary people and those who saw its arrival by the hand of constituted authority—in this case, by the actions of the slaves themselves or by those of the American president. Despite the biting tone, this confrontation did not have the edge of later invective that would ridicule the slaves' incompetence or denounce President Lincoln as a cunning but committed racist.[3]

The argument did not die but continued to roll through American history. In the early twenty-first century, it reemerged in popular culture in Steven Spielberg's award-winning film *Lincoln*. While no one could accuse Spielberg of "desiring to create bad feelings against the Government," *Lincoln* focused on what he believed to be the signal moment in freedom's arrival in the United States: the 1864 congressional debate over the passage of the Thirteenth Amendment. His film reached an audience of millions. Most Americans, at least most white Americans, took Spielberg at his word. Lincoln the president was the Great Emancipator.

If Spielberg's Lincoln-centered argument for emancipation provides a modern analogue to Edward Stoeber's horrified reaction to Delany's speech, *Who Abolished Slavery?*—a small book edited by two distinguished historians, Seymour Drescher and Pieter C. Emmer—takes the argument to another level, expanding on the story of emancipation, from the United States to the Atlantic world. The book is built around a long, contentious essay by yet another eminent scholar, João Pedro Marques, entitled "Slave Revolts and the Abolition of Slavery," along with the series of commentaries that followed. Marques makes his point—that slave revolts played but a small role in ending slavery—with unrelenting force. His take-no-prisoners style quickly elevated *Who Abolished Slavery?* to a central place in the debates over emancipation. He challenges not only the scholarship of his opponents, but also their motives.[4]

For Marques, the extirpation of chattel bondage in the United States and other countries was not the black man's business. Rather than being ever ready to challenge their enslavement, the slaves in Marques's account (if one can judge from the frequency of slave revolts) were at least as likely to acquiesce to their enslavement and even collaborate with their masters in maintaining it. From this perspective, slave insurrections were not attempts to destroy slavery but at best efforts by individual slaves to escape, perhaps gain revenge, or just kill whites. Ultimately, the old order was reestablished, in a pattern that Marques describes as "flight, retaliation, and restoration."[5]

Marques concedes that people of African descent, like others, desired to be free; but they had little interest in universal emancipation—a notion of which they had no knowledge and to which they had no commitment. To the extent that slaves played a part in the arrival of freedom, he believes, their role was narrowly self-interested. Few slaves risked all for a world free of slaves. Given a choice between universal freedom and some improvement in their daily life—shorter hours, larger rations, more time with their families—slaves, according to Marques, nearly always chose the latter. Once they gained their own freedom—as maroons or free people of color—they often became slaveholders themselves.[6]

From Marques's perspective, the great source of abolition was to be found not in the slave quarters but in the legislative halls and executive suites of the European and Euro-American opponents of slavery. In Marques's melodramatic language, "The disappearance of slavery . . . had been achieved not so much through the daggers of black Spartacuses . . . but by the enlightened will of the masters," supported by the even more enlightened will of white Europeans and Euro-Americans. Their job was made easier by the aversion of white people "to the iniquity and brutality of slavery."[7] Their material interests had long suppressed their sympathy for the slaves, but as those material interests dissipated, the basic humanistic—read, antislavery—sensibility emerged and slavery tottered.

The revolution in Saint-Domingue—where black people not only destroyed slavery but also created a republic dedicated to the worldwide destruction of chattel bondage—might be considered the great exception to Marques's understanding of the role of slaves and former slaves. Marques, however, is quick to dismiss the Haitian Revolt as a wrongheaded and counterproductive form of emancipation. Rather than advance the cause of freedom, it sparked a backlash, which frightened even the most stalwart opponents of slavery and fueled hostility to the movement toward freedom. Such abhorrent ideas did not just happen, but were made to happen by what Marques demeaned as "twisted ideology" purveyed by ideologues—an inexplicable and distorted desire to imbue black people "with an antislavery consciousness." For Marques, black people were failures as emancipators: damned if they did (as in Saint-Domingue) and damned if they did not (as in their choice to improve small aspects of their daily life, rather than risk all for freedom).[8]

THE LONG EMANCIPATION challenges both perspectives: the popular view of emancipation in the United States that emerged from Stoeber's or Spielberg's heroic Lincoln, and Marques's interpretation of the Atlantic-wide scholarship that disparaged the actions of enslaved blacks and other people of color. It is an effort to escape the seemingly endless battle between, on the one hand, history understood as the product of the constituted authority emanating from the top, and, on the other, the movement of people acting from the ground up.

The Long Emancipation emphasizes that freedom's arrival was the product not of a moment or a man, but of a process in which many participated—in the case of the United States, a near-century-long process. The demise of slavery was not so much a proclamation as a movement; not so much an occasion as a complex history with multiple players and narratives. Moreover, having characterized the structure of freedom's arrival, *The Long Emancipation* recognizes the four elements that together are always part of the dynamic of slavery's demise.

The first is the primacy of black people, free and slave. Their opposition derived from slavery's denial of their humanity, a denial that was the essence of chattel bondage. From the beginning of emancipation in the flames of the American Revolution to slavery's final demise in the ashes of the Civil War, experience and interest placed black people at the center of the movement for universal freedom. Without their resistance to captivity and without evidence that the enslaved preferred freedom, there could be no movement against slavery. That slaves stood against slavery was irrefutable proof that abolition was possible and not just a reformers' fancy, as slaveowners continually claimed.

Second, in raising the question of African-American emancipation, black people perforce opened the question of their status in freedom and, with it, questions of citizenship and its attributes. If black people were not to be slaves, what exactly would they be? The debate over the future standing of liberated black people led in only one direction, as black people insisted that freedom was a consequence of slavery's destruction.

Third, black people in the United States not only raised the question of their post-emancipation standing, but answered it as well, drawing on their commitment to ideals articulated in the Declaration of Independence and in biblical precepts of evangelical Christianity. The coincidence of the growth of the free black population with that of the American nation connected their status to the notion of freedom articulated in the Declaration of Independence and in the various state charters. Since the free black population grew simultaneously with a nation formally committed to a society based on liberty and equality, black people adopted it as their ideal and became its most steadfast defenders. Nothing seemed more natural to people of color than that all Americans should be equal.

The linkage between slavery's demise and the first three elements of the history of emancipation in the United States leads logically from the arrival of freedom to freedom's meaning—the fourth element. This derives not so much from the history of freedom as from the history of slavery. Undoing slavery required every bit as much brutality as the making of slavery. Lincoln came to appreciate this when he declared in his second inaugural address that justice would not be achieved until the "wealth piled by the bondsman's two hundred and fifty years of unrequited toil shall be sunk, and until every drop of blood drawn with the lash shall be paid by another drawn with the sword."[9] Violence was inherent in the process.

The Long Emancipation weaves these four distinctive characteristics of emancipation into a larger account of the coming of freedom. It is not a full history of abolition in the United States, but offers a framework by which that history might be constructed.

I

The Near-Century-Long
Demise of Slavery

THE SEASON OF emancipation is upon us. The sesquicentennials of the Emancipation Procla- mation and the Thirteenth Amendment have prompted much discussion about the arrival of uni- versal freedom in the United States. Yet, while both events are well worthy of commemoration, they might also be occasions to reconsider the single- minded focus on the wartime destruction of slavery, whether in print, on the small screen, or on the big screen—most powerfully in Steven Spielberg's *Lin- coln*.[1] Slavery's demise might better be understood as a near-century-long process in the United States, entwined with an even longer transatlantic struggle, rather than the work of a moment, even if that mo- ment was a great civil war. To put this another way, emancipation began long before January 1, 1863, and of course continued after it.

Slavery in the United States came apart in pieces. Despite every effort of slaveholders and their allies to make the system of chattel bondage airtight by denying black people access to freedom, slavery proved a leaky vessel. Enslaved black men and women wanted out of bondage, and they found numerous exits prior to the Civil War, with its special Articles of War, Confiscation Acts, congressional legislation, presidential edicts, and the definitive constitutional amendment.

To begin, some Africans arrived in North America prior to the advent of chattel bondage and eluded the snare of enslavement. They and their descendants shared freedom, however imperfect, with other Americans.[2] Among the enslaved, numerous black men and women gained their freedom by successful flight, self-purchase, freedom suits, state-sponsored emancipations, or liberation by individual owners. Prior to the Civil War, the largest group of enslaved African Americans exited slavery in the decades following the American Revolution through a glacially slow process known as "post-nati emancipation," whereby the children born to en-slaved women would be free after a specified date (*post nati* is Latin for "born after").[3] At the same time, Revolutionary ideals of freedom and equality encouraged states of the upper South to expand access to freedom by loosening the regulations gov-erning manumission and freedom suits.[4]

At the end of the eighteenth century, a counter-revolution challenged and, in some places, reversed these open policies that allowed black people access to freedom, constraining the liberty of black free people.[5] But when the opportunity arose, black people were quick to claim it. A second war with Britain, beginning in 1812, allowed another 5,000 to find their way to freedom.[6] And in the years that fol-lowed, black people continued to slip their shackles, so that by the middle years of the nineteenth century the slave South was leaking like a sieve. Slaves fled northward to the free states and Canada; south-ward to Mexico, the Bahamas, and the Caribbean; and at various times across the Atlantic. Not a few slaves emancipated themselves by finding refuge in maroon colonies in Florida, Louisiana, Virginia, and elsewhere within the South, and others found safety on the open sea.[7] Their numbers are hard to gauge. The best recent estimate is that slaves escaped at a rate of 1,000 to 5,000 per year between 1830 and 1860.[8] By 1860, the numerous and diverse exits from slavery had produced a "visible" free black population totaling more than half a million in the United States.[9]

After the outbreak of the Civil War in 1861, the leaks increased exponentially as slaves fled in droves, mostly to Union lines. With expanding opportunities to escape, few waited for the proclamation of January 1, 1863, and neither did Lincoln's administration. The federal government had been freeing slaves for more than a year prior to the issuance of the Emancipation Proclamation, and it would free more thereafter.[10]

On their own, the leaks did not destroy slavery. By the middle of the nineteenth century, the nearly four million enslaved African Americans had made the United States the largest slave society in the world. But neither were the leaks a minor irritant that could be dismissed as a part of the slaveholders' cost of doing business. Instead, they were a pervasive disturbance that infuriated the masters precisely because they threatened both the material and ideological foundation upon which the slave regime rested. They shook the slaveowners' carefully constructed defense of chattel bondage, affirming the antislavery argument in both North and South.

By the middle of the nineteenth century, the seepage had grown, as slaves left the South—particularly the border South—by every imaginable conveyance. They traveled by foot, coach, rail, and boat. Some were mailed in boxes; men disguised themselves as women, and women as men. They fled on their own or en masse, aided by friends and relatives or sometimes by agents of the Underground Railroad.[11] The outflow unnerved slaveholders, who lost not only valuable property but also their confidence in slave loyalty. The resulting instability dissolved the masters' paternalist fictions, along with their beliefs about the social order that had once seemed natural and unquestioned. For their part, black people became more certain that they could free themselves and create a slaveless world.

Still, Americans have tended to view these liberations as separate and distinct from the grand finale of freedom's arrival, the massive Civil War that drove a stake through the heart of chattel bondage. In producing the iconic documents of emancipation and the equally iconic figure of the Great Emancipator, the Civil War remains—in the minds of most people—the singular site of American freedom.

A war that killed three-quarters of a million soldiers and sailors, destroyed billions of dollars' worth of property, and martyred a beloved president provided reason enough to consecrate it as the site of slavery's destruction. The statues, memorial parks, holidays, and other totems of national memory confirm the popular embrace of the wartime emancipation narrative. Even those who recognize—and celebrate—the other sites of black liberty acknowledge the singularity of the Civil War. While wars in general, at least in the American context, have served as solvents of slavery, the emancipatory effects of the Civil War stand apart from those of earlier conflicts. Thus, historians see the antebellum upsurge of slave flight—often aided by increasingly politicized free black communities—and the growth of an organized movement against slavery as a prologue to the final act, not as the play itself. The notion that emancipation was a product of the Civil War is so tightly woven into the fabric of American history that it is hard to imagine the cloth might be cut differently.

UNDERSTANDING the destruction of slavery in the United States not as a single climactic event but as a long process that stretched across a near-century provides a useful and perhaps fuller appreciation of the reality of emancipation. Freedom's arrival was not the work of a moment but the product of movement; it was a process, rather than an occasion.[12]

Taking the long view of slavery's demise broadens and deepens the discussion of who freed the slaves. It places the debate over the roles of President Lincoln, Congress, the Union army, the slaves themselves, and the allied communities of former slaves and descendants of slaves in a broader context, restoring a sense of contingency and undermining the aura of inevitability that attaches itself to a winning cause. The opponents of slavery often argued that history or providence was on their side, but they did not passively wait while history did its work or providence intervened. The goal of a general emancipation, seemingly obvious in retrospect, emerged over time and was only one of the goals the opponents of slavery set for themselves.

The long view exposes with particular clarity the essence of the case against slavery. The bedrock principles on which emancipation rested, often blurred when placed in the context of the shifting tactics and strategies that the opponents of slavery necessarily adopted, appear in sharper focus. Policies changed not only to meet new circumstances, but also to address the masters' ever-shifting defenses in their day-to-day conflicts. The long view reveals the core of abolitionist support: those advocates of universal freedom whose opposition to slavery never wavered. In the end, emancipation—like other victorious causes—had many friends. But that was not true at the beginning or for most of its history. Viewing the process of emancipation over the course of a near-century identifies those men and women who arrived early and stayed late, as well as the more numerous bystanders.

For similar reasons, the long view suggests the many ways in which emancipation in the United States was at one with the demise of slavery elsewhere in the Atlantic world, where the struggle took many different forms. Just as Britain's parliamentary Emancipation Act (1833) cannot be seen apart from Quaker manifestos of the 1750s, just as

Cuba's 1880 Ley de Patronato is closely linked to its Moret Law (1870), and just as Brazil's Golden Law (1888) connects to the Anglo-Brazilian Slave Trade Treaty (1826), so the millions of enslaved men and women freed by wartime emancipation throughout America cannot be separated from the nineteen slaves liberated by Vermont's 1777 constitution.[13]

The *longue durée* of emancipation provides a reminder that significant social change requires commitments sometimes extending over generations, and that while the terrain of struggle continually changes, the final goal does not. In the case of the struggle over slavery, the long view connects the arrival of freedom with the post-emancipation standing of former slaves, hence with the debate over citizenship and its attributes, among them race, as well as with the confrontation over property-in-man that made some people rich. At every turn, the coincidence between blackness and slavery necessitated the creation of a new relationship. Emancipation, in short, was a critical moment in the history of racialization—and it, too, was a long process. The era of Reconstruction, generally attached to the post–Civil War struggle under that name, began as the first Africans and African

Americans exited slavery and staked their claim to freedom.

But while the long perspective on emancipation clarifies and sharpens understanding, it can also distort. For one thing, it encourages the notion that the demise of slavery was a linear, progressive process—frequently endowed by providence—in which liberty marched ever forward, even in the face of stout opposition. In his *Notes on the State of Virginia* (1781), Thomas Jefferson conceded slavery's decline and imagined its inevitable end, observing, "The spirit of the master is abating, that of the slave rising from the dust . . . preparing, under the auspices of heaven, for a total emancipation." As with so many other Jeffersonian contentions respecting African-American slavery and freedom, the master of Monticello was at best partially correct. Although the slaves' demand for freedom was growing steadily at the end of the eighteenth century, the spirit of the master—including his own mastership—was hardly abating. Jefferson's opposition to slavery waned over time, if not in principle then certainly in practice. He held more slaves at his death in 1826 than when he had penned his *Notes* some fifty years earlier. As he aged, Jefferson dissociated himself from even the most cautious proposals to end slavery. He failed to free his own slaves, save for his kin, and deferred the arrival of universal freedom to an indefinite future.[14] For the mass of Southern slaveholders, the commitment to the system of chattel bondage that made them rich and oft-times defined them increased during the next eighty years. American slavery would be stronger in 1800 than it had been in 1775, and stronger still in 1860 than it had been in 1800.

Yet as slavery advanced, so did its opposition. The parallel trajectories of slavery and antislavery pose critical questions about the nature of their relationship. Did the Quakers' petitions to an unreceptive first Congress, the advent of the African colonization movement, the publication of William Lloyd Garrison's *Liberator*, the organization of the Liberty Party, or John Brown's raid on Harper's Ferry lead slave masters to escalate the defense of slavery, or did such advocacy merely expose their long-established positions? Likewise, did the enactment of the Southwest Ordinance, the passage of the Fugitive Slave Act, or the announcement of the *Dred Scott* decision incite new antislavery activities or reveal time-honored beliefs? Struggling with these chicken-and-egg questions (Who were the aggressors in the slavery wars? How can we distinguish between newly established positions and the hardening of older ones?), historians have pushed the Southern support for slavery and the Northern commitment to free labor further back in time. Sentiments that were once attributable to John C. Calhoun or William Lloyd Garrison in the mid-nineteenth century have been discerned fifty years earlier.[15] In this seemingly timeless ubiquity, a prime mover in the challenge to or defense of slavery disappears. Slavery and antislavery appear to feed upon each other in a dialectical fashion—a conclusion that may be judicious but is hardly satisfying. At best, the dénouement of the conflict between slavery and antislavery affirmed that emancipation's road was long and bumpy.

Noting this, historians of emancipation have paid a good deal of attention to the bumps, those moments in which the movement for universal freedom switched gears, seeing them as harbingers of distinctive stages or periods in the long struggle against slavery. They have distinguished between "emancipationists" and "abolitionists," not only according to their principles (gradualists versus immediatists) but also according to their geographical bases (Pennsylvania versus Massachusetts).[16] The transformation of the movement for universal freedom—from elitist to equalitarian, legalistic to moralistic, secular to evangelical, religious to political, and nonviolent to violent, finally ending triumphantly in the bloody crescendo of civil war—has provided a framework for understanding the long emancipation in the United States.[17]

The changes had many sources. The geographic growth of the United States, the democratization of American politics, the new place accorded to women, and the expansion of the market economy, along with the transformation of religious life and the growing literacy of the American people—all reshaped the war against slavery. So, too, did changes within the antislavery movement. But whatever the source of change, when one divides the evolution of the antislavery movement into different periods during which opposition to slavery took distinctive forms, each manifesting its own particular ideologies and rhetoric, strategies and tactics, leaders, cadres, and constituencies, this approach has its limitations. It has provoked endless debates over the roles of different individuals or groups: the primacy of

William Lloyd Garrison over Theodore Dwight
Weld, evangelicals over politicians, and, most recently, whites over blacks. It has launched a search
for previously unknown proponents of freedom,
whose contribution had not been fully acknowledged. The intramural jousting has greatly expanded
knowledge of the antislavery movement, and a host
of new men and women have come to the fore. Yet
the task of gaining a sense of the whole remains
incomplete.

Understanding emancipation as a series of as-
cending steps that culminated in slavery's demise
leaves in place the familiar linear march of freedom.
Although played out within a more complex ma-
trix, this story closely resembles the old. Exhibiting
various strengths and weaknesses to meet the slave
masters' challenge, the diverse opponents of slavery
pressed their case, often advancing the cause but
always falling short of the final goal. When one
failed—say, legalistic gradualism, with its tempered end to slavery—another replaced it. But the
replacement—say, evangelical immediatism, with
its call for instantaneous abolition—proved no more
successful in achieving its stated aim, so it, too,
gave way. This view not only compartmentalizes

the history of emancipation, but again reinforces the Whiggish, or progressive, teleology of freedom's arrival. The history of emancipation becomes something like that of a holometabolous bug which metamorphoses from egg to larva, and then to a pupa—peeling off the dried husks of different stages—before emerging as a beautiful butterfly (read: freedom). In short, it poses many of the same problems that weaken the linear march-of-freedom story.

A close look at the step-like stages that historians have ascribed to the long history of emancipation quickly strips them of their singularity and, instead, reveals many commonalities. The seemingly distinctive stages speak to differences in tactics and strategies that were repeated in endless variation as the opponents of slavery gained traction. The religious principle that all are equal in the sight of God was a critical impetus to abolition as it emerged from Quaker meetinghouses in the mid-eighteenth century. While opposition to slavery later moved to the hustings and then to the counting-houses, the religious impetus never disappeared. Likewise, the belief that the state—both the local and national governments—could play a critical role in abolishing slavery was as central to the thinking of the Pennsylvania Society for Promoting the Abolition of Slavery in the 1790s as it was to that of the Republican Party in the 1850s, even if the two organizations had a different understanding of the role of the state. Similarly, lawyers—who stood at the forefront of the initial assault on slavery in the immediate post-Revolutionary era—continued to be of central importance in the 1840s and 1850s, emerging as critical to the formulation of the movement against slavery. In short, the means that were employed to attack slavery did not develop sequentially but functioned simultaneously, as the opponents of slavery warred on all fronts. To a remarkable degree, antislavery sentiment remained constant over the long haul.

THE KEY TO THE history of emancipation in the United States cannot be found in a series of escalating stages that marked the ever-widening assault on property-in-man or the changing styles of antislavery activism. Instead, it can best be revealed by examining the elements—four in number—that shaped the long struggle for universal freedom. Although played out against the ever-changing circumstances of American life, these four omni-present constituents of emancipation's long history provide the essentials for understanding the arrival of universal freedom in the United States.[18]

First, the long emancipation centered on the res-olute commitment of a few men and women—most of them black slaves, along with former slaves and the descendants of slaves—to end slavery and create a slaveless world. Their experience and memories of captivity propelled them to the front ranks of the movement, if only by providing clear evidence that they—the enslaved—refused to accept their en-slavement. In their opposition to slavery and their demands for its immediate end, they were the most insistent and determined. Slavery's denial of hu-manity and its extraordinary exploitation touched them as it did no others. Their opposition was di-rect and personal, for they had felt the sting of the master's lash, witnessed the destruction of their fam-ilies and communities, and experienced the mali-cious condescension that was heaped upon people of African descent. And if they had not directly expe-rienced slavery's weight, they knew that they *could* experience it, because no black person—despite the differences within the black community—was safe in a world that equated blackness and bondage. "We are one people, chained together. We are one people—one in general complexion, one in common degradation, one in common estimation," declared the delegates to the 1848 Colored National Convention. Experience and interest placed black people at the center of the movement for universal freedom. Without their resistance to captivity, and without proof certain that the enslaved preferred freedom, there could be no movement against slavery.[19]

To put this another way, free blacks' claims for respectability, their ability to improve themselves, and their ability to escape the degradation of chattel bondage all rested on opposition to slavery. Apologists for slavery depicted black people as irredeemably inferior precisely because this portrayal undercut the antislavery argument. The status of servitude became, in itself, a justification for the denial of rights to free blacks.[20]

Second, raising the question of African-American emancipation perforce opened the issue of the status of black people in freedom, and therefore the question of citizenship and its attributes. If black people were not to be slaves, what exactly would they be? Dependent, disorderly proletarians with no stake in the social order? Independent proprietors with standing as citizens? The choice would tell all. It was impossible to imagine the future standing of black people without becoming entangled in matters of citizenship—and then race. From the first, when abolitionists spoke of liberty, they spoke of *equal* liberty.[21]

The third element is closely related to the second. No history of emancipation in the United States can be complete without an appreciation of the depth of African Americans' commitment to the fulfillment of the Declaration of Independence via the creation of a multiracial republic. But American slavery was racial slavery. On whatever ground the struggle over slavery was fought, the post-emancipation status of black people and the matter of racial equality came to the fore. The challenge to racial slavery necessarily evoked the question of racial freedom, and so the matter of race and the relationship between whites and blacks emerged simultaneously with any discussion of emancipation. The debate sometimes focused on post-emancipation indentures, and especially on the education deemed suitable for former slaves. It also addressed access to the suffrage and the rights of free blacks to travel freely, sit on juries, bear arms, and serve in the militia. The debate extended to the ability of black people literally to sit anywhere—on an omnibus, railroad car, or boat—attend the theater, stay in a hotel, or even marry whom they chose. This was true both in the North and in the South, both in the post-Revolutionary emancipations and in the Civil War collapse of bondage. Indeed, it was as true in the larger global struggle against slavery as it was in the United States.[22]

Finally and most inescapably, emancipation was always a violent process, for undoing the violence of enslavement required just as much brutality as the creation of chattel bondage, if not more. Lincoln, as noted above, believed that slavery's lash would be repaid with freedom's sword. Yet the violence that accompanied emancipation stemmed from more than the rational rebalancing of the blood of the oppressor and the blood of the liberator.[23] It was fueled by the searing rage of slaves and former slaves who saw their opportunities for a decent life taken from them, and by that of the masters who fabricated and defended an equally emotive commitment to a way of life based upon slave labor.

THE PRIMACY OF black people provides a beginning for any discussion of the long emancipation. Asserting the centrality of black people in the struggle to end slavery in no way denies the principled commitment, extraordinary courage, and deep sacrifice of others to the antislavery cause, which can rightly been seen as the first interracial social movement. Such recognition goes beyond the obligatory bow to the men and women who were the slaves' best friends at a time when slaves had few friends. Emancipation would have been delayed far beyond its 1865 end—perhaps, as Abraham Lincoln mused in the Lincoln-Douglas debates, well into the twentieth century—without the actions of white abolitionists. No one knew this better than the white opponents of slavery who were viewed as instigators of slaves' insurrectionary activism. Yet William Lloyd Garrison, often seen as the mastermind behind Nat Turner's rebellion, was aware of a deeper truth. "The slaves need no incentives at our hands," he famously declared. "They will find them in their stripes."[24] White abolitionists provided something essential in their interactions with blacks, both black abolitionists and ordinary black men and women: if a multiracial community was to be found in the United States, it was to be found within the abolitionist community.

This reality does not minimize the fact that the vast majority of black and white Americans—and black and white abolitionists—lived in different worlds, which themselves had developed from slavery and from the allied structures of white supremacy. Material differences in wealth that spawned differences in education and aspirations elevated whites, imbuing them with a sense that they were the blacks' defenders, protectors, and benefactors but not their colleagues and comrades. Such condescension manifested itself in Samuel Ringgold Ward's lament that all-too-many white opponents of slavery "love the colored man at a distance."[25]

But such patronizing was only one measure of the gap that separated blacks and whites. Differences in their opposition to slavery offered a more accurate measure of the distance between them. White abolitionists focused on the societal damage slavery wrought as it perverted the work ethic, corrupted Christianity, distorted democracy, and twisted the most basic human relations. Black abolitionists decried all of slavery's detrimental effects, but they emphasized the slaves' suffering, the physical and psychological abuse they endured, and the multiple ways slavery denied men and women a normal life, most especially familial life.[26]

These differences made it difficult, if not impossible, for black and white abolitionists to see one another as equals. White abolitionists were making the world anew; blacks were repairing the damage created by the old world. "The friends of the colored people took part in antislavery work as a matter of duty . . . but they were no more likely to believe that Negroes were naturally equal to whites than they were that chalk was cheese," wrote a correspondent to *Frederick Douglass' Paper*. Douglass himself felt the differences. "They talk down here," he wrote to an equally frustrated friend, referring to white abolitionists, "just as if the Anti-Slavery Cause belonged to them—and as if all Anti-Slavery ideas originated with them and that no man has a right to 'peep or mutter' on the subject, who does not hold letters patent from them."[27]

Asserting the primacy of black abolitionists likewise does not deny that many black people did little to aid the struggle for universal freedom, whether because of their indifference, their fear, their feelings of powerlessness, or their active opposition to abolition—a painful reality evidenced by the continual denunciations of African-American apathy and calls for black unity. Slavery, like every system of oppression, could not be sustained without the tacit consent of the oppressed. Not a few slaves sought freedom for themselves and cared little or nothing for their fellows still in bondage. For every Denmark Vesey there was a George Pencil, who gained his freedom by revealing Vesey's plot.[28] Once freed, these black men and women did not look back, and a few passed quickly from slave to slaveowner.[29] The presence of black slaveowners exposes the complex and problematic relationship between resistance to slavery, personal advancement, and principled commitment.

Collaborators were the least of the many problems stemming from black indifference to black freedom struggles. The very circumstances that stoked black opposition to slavery often impeded the ability of black people to work in support of abolition. Acting from the same bedrock opposition to slavery, slave and free black protesters might well settle for less, as they confronted the brutal on-the-ground realities of the slave masters' power. While malingering, tool breaking, flight, arson, sabotage, poisonings, and rebellion spoke of the desire to smash the chains of bondage, most slaves grudgingly accepted—and sometimes welcomed—improvements in their lives in lieu of the risks entailed in reaching for complete freedom. Toussaint L'Ouverture, who came to represent the heroic, complete destruction of slavery, would have settled for much less in the years before slavery's final collapse in Saint-Domingue.[30] In the long history of slavery, most slaves—like Toussaint during his alliance with the slaveholding Spanish—followed the path of expedience, rather than that of the heroic emancipator who draped himself in the tricolor and espoused slavery's utter destruction. Black men and women, like most people, were risk-averse even when taking the greatest of risks. Faced with unpleasant choices, the vast majority—judging rebellion to be futile and perhaps suicidal—found an accommodation that would ameliorate slavery's harsh conditions and open a more certain path to a better life, at least in the short run. Why risk all, when a small gain could be safely achieved?

Enslaved men and women hated their confinement and sought every opportunity to break the shackles that bound them, but opposition to their own enslavement—or even the enslavement of others—did not automatically make them abolitionists. For much of their history—indeed, for much of human history—the notion of a world purged of slavery was simply unimaginable. Abolition, like any other social movement, was rooted in history and confined in time and space. Prior to the American Revolution and its ideology of universal equality, there were few movements to contemplate, let alone to join.[31]

Even as the notion of a slaveless world slowly emerged at the end of the eighteenth century, not all slaves embraced it, either because they judged it—as did most Americans—theoretically unlikely or because, practically, they could not fit it into their understanding of how the world worked. Many slaves, carefully calculating how they might best improve their own condition, stood at their master's side and, in some cases, gained their freedom by informing on slave conspirators, assisting in the capture of slave fugitives, and serving as their owner's ears in the slave quarters.

But although tactical considerations may have caused slaves to accept compromises short of full and immediate freedom, their unalloyed opposition to chattel bondage emerged at the first opportunity. To them, slavery was not merely a political system or an economic contrivance. The purpose of opposing slavery was not to create a more efficient economy, or a more perfect republic, or to win some partisan battle, or to express disdain for haughty masters. Rather, it was part of the slaves' ongoing struggle for full equality that may have begun as an attempt to improve conditions of daily life but that always aimed for recognition of their dignity and the respect accorded a free people.

Among African Americans, those who had gained their freedom—hence escaped the slaveholder's immediate orbit—played a particularly important role in the struggle for freedom. But here, too, the masters' shadow could not be easily escaped. This was particularly true of free people who resided within the portion of American society in which slavery continued to function. (In 1860, the slave South accounted for more than half of the free black population). In the South, as in other slave societies, free people of color—viewed as subversive by definition—found it to their advantage to distance themselves from slaves, as the mere hint of an alliance between free and enslaved blacks could stir the slaveholders' wrath. By speaking, dressing, and deporting themselves differently from slaves, free men and women of color in the South sought to assure masters that they stood apart from slaves, a point made even more forcefully in the cases when they themselves became slaveowners.[32]

Black people in the free states did not carry the burden of their Southern counterparts, free and slave. Residing beyond the slaveholders' immediate grasp, Northern free blacks linked their own fate to that of the slaves and championed the slaves' cause as their own. For many, the tie was direct and personal, since free people of color—often just a step removed from slavery themselves—usually had family and friends locked in bondage. Many were fugitives themselves, so speaking of the slaves' cause as their own came naturally. More than others, they understood that their own freedom depended upon slavery's abolition. H. Ford Douglas, who, like many fugitives (Henry "Box" Brown, Frederick Douglass, Harriet Jacobs), rose from runaway to a position of leadership in the antislavery movement, spoke as much to slaves as to abolitionists when he declared, "You must either free the slaves, or the slaves will free themselves."[33]

When the crisis came, no other Americans—white or black—pressed harder than free blacks for the opportunity to fight the slaveholding enemy, despite risks of enslavement and execution. Their commitment derived from their understanding that as long as the vast majority of white Americans connected blackness and slavery, they, too, would be denied the full rights of Americans. Free African Americans would forever be viewed as unequal where the masses of black people were slaves.[34] Thus, no one more consistently urged the creation of a slave-free world in which all were equal. These men and women would be the yeast in the ferment—the active element that was critical for the growth of abolition.

As the leading edge of the movement against slavery, Northern free blacks drove the opposition to slavery to its logic conclusion: immediate and total abolition. They gave the slaves' oppositional activities a political form, denying the masters' claim that malingering and tool breaking were reflections of African idiocy and indolence, that sabotage represented the mindless thrashings of a primitive people, and that outsiders were the ones who always inspired conspiracies and insurrections. Taking to the pulpit, the podium, the press, they publicized the slaves' refusal to accept slavery (a refusal the masters claimed made no sense, according to their fiction of the happy slave). Without a black public presence, there would be no yeast to raise the bread.[35]

The free black population emerged with the American Revolution and immediately embraced the notions of equality embedded in the Declaration of Independence and evangelical awakenings—hence the second essential element in any understanding of emancipation's long history. After the Revolution, freed people made the commitment to equality their political signature. This touchstone of American nationality and Christian belief became the basic truth that black Americans embraced and that white Americans could not publicly repudiate without surrendering to the charge of hypocrisy. It became the basis for black opposition—and, eventually, all opposition—to slavery, sounding a clarion that echoed through the long history of emancipation between the Revolution and the Civil War. The initial movement for freedom in the Northern states, the long struggle for freedom in the slave South, and the final wartime destruction of slavery all rested on the expectation and demand for equality, meaning access to the tools of citizenship: at a minimum, the right to vote and the ability to earn a living through one's labor.[36] The commitment to equality became the second defining feature of emancipation's long history.[37]

Of course, black people, like others, defined the remarkably elastic notion of equality according to their own lights. Most had no particular attachment to equality in the abstract or as a functioning system of social relations. Among themselves, black people appeared as comfortable with a hierarchical social order and deferential politics as other Americans. Maroon colonies in the United States, as elsewhere, were hierarchical.[38] Much the same was true of black society generally, for the black experience was diverse. As James McCune Smith observed, in his efforts to wrestle with the divisions in the black community, "the main reason we are not united is we are not equally oppressed."[39]

As a matter of political commitment, black Americans generally supported the parties of the right—the political organizations most closely allied with hierarchies of status, wealth, achievement, and sometimes birth—whose attachment to class rather than racial distinctions made them an attractive ally. In the early years of the nineteenth century, when some free black men acquired the suffrage, they generally voted Federalist and later Whig. African-American society—slave and free—was riven with hierarchies of wealth, education, occupation, status, and color, among other markers of difference. Who should vote and who should have access to the marketplace was a matter of difference among black people, just as it was among other Americans.[40]

The challenge to African-American slavery necessarily evoked the matter of race, and the relationship between whites and blacks emerged simultaneously with any discussion of emancipation. The Declaration of Independence made equality normative, leaving only one logical rationale for denying freedom to any people: namely, that they were not fully human.[41] The matter of universal freedom was thus allied with questions of origin, color, and the character of other attributes, physical and mental, that presumably distinguished white from black. Such explanations could not stand on their own. Neither the Declaration nor the Bible—the two great sources of authority for the American people—could justify such a claim. The Declaration's words left no room for exceptions, nor did the Bible's emphasis on the unity of Creation. To find exceptions to these *ur*-texts of American nationality took considerable intellectual work, and that work intensified as the possibility of universal freedom grew. History had to be rewritten, the story of Creation revised, and human physiognomy reconceived, for the contradictions were manifest.

The discussion of emancipation—even the smallest suggestion of emancipation—elevated the significance of race, ratcheting up both the volume and level of debate over freedom's meaning. As the struggle for universal freedom gained in intensity, the gulf grew between those who embraced the Declaration's literal meaning in order to create an interracial democracy and those who divided humanity into white and black, and parsed the attributes of freedom along racial lines. James Forten, a leader of Philadelphia's African-American community, staked his claim to equality on the founding documents of American nationality. "Whatever measures are adopted subversive of this inestimable privilege, are in direct violation of the letter and spirit of our Constitution, and become subject to the animadversion of all." "All men are born equally free," he went on, and the "law knows no distinction."[42] The long history of emancipation was thus, at the same time, a chapter in the long history of race. As the movement on behalf of emancipation grew, so too did the debate over the making and remaking of race, its definitions and meaning.

The final feature of emancipation's long history was the ubiquity of violence. The reference here is not to the great explosions that echo through American history—bleeding Kansas, John Brown's raid, or the Civil War itself—but to the ceaseless carnage that manifested itself in every confrontation between master and slave. In the clash of powerful material interests and deeply held beliefs, slaveholders and their numerous allies did not give way easily. Beginning with abolition in the North—although this was generally described as a peaceful process imbued with the ethos of Quaker quietism and legislative and judicial activism—the movement for universal freedom was one of violent, bloody conflict that left a trail of destroyed property, broken bones, traumatized men and women, and innumerable lifeless bodies. It was manifested in direct confrontations, kidnappings, pogroms, riots, insurrections, and finally open warfare. Usually, the masters and their allies—with their monopoly on violence—perpetrated much of the carnage. To challenge that monopoly required force, often deadly force; when the opponents of slavery struck back with violence of their own, the attacks and counterattacks escalated. The pattern held in the North, where there were few slaves, and in the South, where there were many. When the Civil War arrived and the war for union became a war for freedom, violence was raised to another level, but the precedent had been long established.

Over the course of the near-century from the New England abolitions to the ratification of the Thirteenth Amendment, the four distinctive elements—the centrality of black people, the commitment to universal freedom, the necessity of racial equality, and the ubiquity of violence—wove the history of emancipation into a single piece. Their interconnections give the history of universal freedom in the United States its special character.

2

Sounding the Egalitarian Clarion

"ALL MEN ARE CREATED equal." By any measure, this was an extraordinary statement, certainly for a society in which hierarchy was the norm governing nearly every social relationship: man-woman, husband-wife, master-apprentice, and, of course, master-slave. It was even more extraordinary coming from a slaveholder born to the Virginia gentry. Nonetheless, Thomas Jefferson—asserting the American claim to independence—declared the maxim to be "self-evident."[1]

Whatever else could be said of equality at the end of the eighteenth century, self-evident it was not. If, like Jefferson, some Americans subscribed to that notion in the abstract, it had little to do with life as lived. Most people, certainly those in the upper orders to which Jefferson belonged, rejected its practical application out of hand, dismissing the Declaration's ringing phrase as a rhetorical flourish employed—brilliantly from the perspective of the Patriots, cynically from that of the Loyalists—to rally Americans to the cause of independence.

But if the elite disparaged the egalitarian ideal, those at the bottom of American society embraced it, none more enthusiastically than the nearly one million enslaved Africans and African Americans and the small, but growing, free black population. Black people—like millions of other subordinate people—seized Jefferson's self-evident truth and made it their own. For some, it only reinforced the assurances of spiritual equality offered by religious radicals who found a spark of divinity in every soul, and by evangelical Christians who preached that all were equal in God's eyes.[2] For many, perhaps most, who knew something of the world and had observed their "masters" without the trappings of superiority, Jefferson's notion was only common sense. It provided an antidote to the allegations of inferiority that weighed heavily upon them.

Others shared this egalitarian persuasion. Whether these beliefs emerged from the natural-rights philosophy of the Enlightenment, from the theology of radical Protestant sectarians, or from the emerging sensitivity to the commonalities of human nature, the confluence of egalitarian ideas and revolutionary experience produced a heady mixture that the American people adopted as their first principle. As the Declaration became the touchstone of American nationality, men and women—especially those confined to the margins of American society, such as religious dissenters, laboring people, women of all ranks, and of course enslaved and free people of color—employed Jefferson's self-evident truth to fulfill the nation's promise.[3] While the power of the egalitarian ideal waxed and waned over the next century—indeed, over the entire course of American history—it had a particularly powerful resonance among black Americans.

The commitment to human equality was at the heart of nearly every official assertion of republican independence. "[A]ll men are by nature equally free and independent, and have certain inherent rights, of which, when they enter into a state of society, they cannot, by any compact, deprive or divest their posterity; namely, the enjoyment of life and liberty," read the Virginia Bill of Rights of 1776. The Massachusetts Constitution, promulgated four years later, echoed it: "All men are born free and equal, and have certain natural, essential, and unalienable rights; among which may be the right of enjoying and defending their lives and liberties." Likewise the New Hampshire Constitution of 1784: "All men are born equally free and independent; therefore . . . have certain natural and essential, and inherent rights; among which are enjoying and defending life and liberty." Incorporating the Declaration into their own work, some state constitution makers found it difficult to achieve the simplicity and eloquence of Jefferson's original formulation. To remedy that problem, a few—like those in New York—lifted Jefferson's phrasing and transcribed it verbatim into their own founding declarations.[4] In its various forms, the rhetoric of equality became the language of American nationality.

The struggle for universal freedom in mainland North America had many sources, some of which extended far back into the seventeenth century, but it began in earnest with the legitimation of the idea of equality by the Declaration of Independence and the biblical precepts of the evangelical awakenings. Thereafter, its history would follow a variety of courses. Like a mighty torrent, it would sometimes roar ahead; but it often stopped suddenly, as if meeting a logjam and would roll backward, searching for a new channel, which in turn might prove to be a dead end or might allow the stream to flow freely again. The history of emancipation would be characterized by endless complexity, pervasive ambiguity, no small measure of irony, and not a few contradictions, as principle and opportunism met in strange combinations. But its point of origin would continue to inform its development.

By making equality, not hierarchy, the normative principle upon which all society rested, Americans put the institution of slavery at risk. Slavery offended the Revolution's highest principle: that privilege—whether understood in terms of honor or in terms of material reward—must be earned rather than ascribed. Like monarchs and aristocrats, slaveholders lived parasitically off the labor of others, violating the essence of the new nation's republican creed. Over time, the contradiction between the nation's commitment to human equality and the presence of human bondage became more and more blatant. Opponents of slavery evoked it regularly as they attacked slavery. "Can we expect to triumph over G[reat] Britain, to get free ourselves until we let those go free under us?" asked an attorney (who concealed his identity) making the case for his client's freedom.[5] As underscoring the contradictions became a more regular feature of the revolutionary rhetoric, white Americans, with Southerners in the lead but many Northerners not far behind, found in the impoverished and dependent circumstances of black people reason enough to deny them an equal place in the Republic. Some went further: they parsed humanity and distributed its finer attributes in unequal portions, claiming that people of African descent lacked the qualities necessary for a free citizenry. Still, even in the face of opposition, black people found the idea of equality—whether derived from the sacred or from the secular—a useful tool for exerting pressure on the institution of slavery. At first, they eroded its edges. In time, they would destroy the entire edifice of chattel bondage and the society that relied upon it.

Slavery everywhere had begun in violence, rested on violence, and nearly always ended in violence.[6] This was even more true in a society that had been formed in the throes of a revolution. Although the members of the Society of Friends had started to divest themselves of their slaves peacefully in the middle of the eighteenth century, tramping armies set in motion by the War for American Independence provided the occasion for the first mass exodus from slavery. The confusion that followed in the army's wake allowed thousands of black men and women to seize their freedom. Some separated themselves from their owners in the wartime turmoil, while others found welcome havens in the encampments of both belligerents.[7]

The British—first Lord Dunmore in 1775, and then General-in-Chief Henry Clinton in 1779—were the first to institute a formal policy by which an enslaved man could exchange military service for freedom. Before long, the Patriots—often acting more from desperation than from principle—did the same. The number of black soldiers began to multiply. "[N]o regiment is to be seen," observed a Hessian soldier serving with the British, "in which there are no negroes in abundance." It seemed that slavery was being "extinguished" by what President Lincoln would later call "mere friction and abrasion . . . of the war."[8]

Finding divisions within the slaveholding class and playing one side against the other, black men leveraged their freedom as soldiers. But others—women as well as men—likewise secured their liberty on the battlefield, even if they never picked up a musket. Rather, they traded their labor working as teamsters, boatmen, seamstresses, and domestics, doing much of the dirty work of war in exchange for freedom. Some labored in an official capacity, as guides and pioneers, filling a familiar role at the base of the chain of command. Most made ad hoc arrangements with common soldiers—Patriot or Loyalist—beyond the purview of their commanders, pitching tents, cleaning camps, and cooking food, as the circumstances of war transformed tasks common to life in slavery into a means of access to freedom. On occasion, they, too, picked up a gun.[9]

For the most part, black men and women caught up in the maelstrom of war needed no lengthy explanations to justify abandoning their owners in favor of freedom. But when the opportunities arose, they mobilized the language of equality in the cause of their own liberty. As they did, the courthouse and the state house also became sites of liberation.[10]

Black Americans seized the initiative in the judicial war against slavery. Wherever they had access to the law, the number of freedom suits swelled,

and the struggle for universal liberty burst onto the courtroom floor as black people aggressively pressed their case.[11] These suits drew upon furtive knowledge of relationships long hidden by the massive expansion of slavery during the late seventeenth and early eighteenth centuries. Typical of many similar legal battles was the case regarding descendants of Eleanor Nell, also known as "Irish Nell," a white woman who had been indentured to Charles Calvert, the third Lord Baltimore, in mid-seventeenth-century Maryland. In 1681, Eleanor had married Charles Butler, an enslaved black man, and in so doing had become a slave for life under a 1664 Maryland law. Although the law was later repealed, her children and her children's children nonetheless inherited Nell's bonded status. In 1770, nearly a century later, the new circumstances of the Revolution enabled them to attain their freedom. Nell's descendants—her great-grandchildren, or perhaps great-great-grandchildren—drawing upon family lore, sued for their freedom on the grounds that their ancestor was a white woman. They brought their suit in the Maryland courts, which allowed hearsay testimony and free-black testimony. When elderly neighbors—white and black—confirmed the ancient history, the Butlers went free on the basis of hearsay testimony.[12]

The Butlers soon inspired many other litigants, who claimed freedom on the basis of a white or Native-American foremother. In 1786 and again in 1787, other members of the Butler clan claiming descent from Irish Nell were in the courts, many beyond the borders of Maryland. Such actions deepened understanding of the law within the slave community, creating a pool of practical legal knowledge—what historians have come to call a "legal culture"—that enslaved men and women drew upon when the opportunity arose. Common knowledge of their familial ties going back generations, combined with increasing legal sophistication, allowed black men and women to articulate their claim of freedom in a language that attracted sympathetic lawyers to their cause. While white attorneys carried the burden in court, the slaves' legal culture—and their courage in daring to challenge slavery—provided the hook upon which lawyers could hang their cases. As enslaved black men and women exerted pressure on the judicial system, courts in some locales liberalized the terms of freedom suits, allowing black people to testify and to make use of hearsay evidence, which increased their chances of success.[13]

Once in court, these suits could take on a life of their own, as demonstrated by the case of James Somerset, an American slave whose owner, Charles Stewart, had purchased him in Boston and taken him to England. When Stewart threatened to return him to America, Somerset fled; after he was recaptured, he sued for his freedom with the aid of British abolitionists. In 1772, in a landmark decision, the presiding judge, Lord Mansfield, accepted the argument of Somerset's abolitionist counsel—namely, that the "air of England is too pure for a slave to breathe in." Slavery, the attorney explained, violated man's natural rights and could exist only within the purview of local law. Once the slave was outside that jurisdiction, his or her condition reverted to freedom. Somerset gained his liberty.[14] That decision, along with the Butler case, opened the door to judicial abolition, which became more pointed as the American mainland colonies contended with the English metropole.

If English air was too pure to allow slavery, what of American air, which Patriots, struggling to free themselves from English tyranny, claimed was even purer? In 1781, Mum Bett—or, as she later called herself, Elizabeth Freeman—sued for her freedom in the western Massachusetts town of Great Barrington. Her suit attracted the attention of Theodore Sedgwick, a local attorney who would later rise to leadership in the Federalist Party and eventually serve as a United States senator. Sedgwick tossed aside the specifics of Mum Bett's case against her owner and instead argued that under the provisions of the new Massachusetts Constitution—"all men are born free and equal"—slavery had no standing in law. When the case reached the state Supreme Court, the justices were already adjudicating a similar freedom suit, the case of a runaway named Quok Walker. They joined the two cases and ruled against the legality of slavery, with Chief Justice William Cushing asserting that slavery was incompatible with "the natural rights of mankind" to freedom and equality that the state constitution guaranteed.[15]

Cushing's verdict—taken by some to be an extension of the Somerset case—eroded chattel bondage in the state. Enslaved black men and women, drawing on their own expanding knowledge of the law, took their owners to court. With the outcome

of such suits a foregone conclusion, slaveholders did not even bother to defend themselves. Eventually, black men and women shortened the process and simply left their owners, setting a precedent that would become a key factor in slavery's demise.[16]

As judicial emancipations doomed slavery in Massachusetts, black people, free and slave, mobilized the egalitarian rhetoric of the Revolution to break the bonds of their enslavement, making pleas—sometimes demands—for freedom. Exposing the hypocrisy manifest in the slaveowners' celebration of universal equality, they turned the Patriots' language against them. "We expect great things from men who have made such a noble stand against the designs of their *fellow-men* to enslave them," petitioned four enslaved black men to the Massachusetts General Court in 1773.[17] They urged—in a manner that sounded more like a taunt than a supplication—that any reordering of the relationship between colonial Americans and their British overlords should begin with a parallel reordering of black Americans and their white overlords.

In the years that followed, the enslaved petitioners dropped their acerbic tone, but their conviction that they should be free only grew. In 1779, black Connecticut petitioners put their case in the simplest terms, asserting that they were "endowed with the same facilities with [as] our masters, and the more we consider the matter, the more we are convinced of our right to be free." They, too, continued to wrap their demand for liberty in the rhetoric of the American colonies' desire for freedom from political bondage. Like the Massachusetts petitioners, they argued that human rights rested upon agreements men entered into voluntarily. "A great number of blacks of this province . . . held in a state of slavery within the bowels of a free and Christian country, have in common with all other men a natural right to our freedoms . . . as we are a freeborn people and have never forfeited this blessing by any compact or agreement," asserted another slave-authored petition the following year. Slowly, legislation calling for abolition wended its way through the Connecticut General Court; it had first been reported out of committee during the 1773 session and had passed both houses during the next session, but never gained full approval. Still, the legislature continued to be bombarded with petitions informed by the very same egalitarian sentiment that Chief Justice

Cushing would eventually employ to doom slavery in Massachusetts.[18]

Under the pressure of such assaults, the support for slavery wavered in New England. The tremors were felt first where slaves were fewest in number and most marginal to the economy. In 1777, Vermont—which just one year earlier had broken away from New York, proclaimed itself a Republic, and then gained recognition as a separate state—ratified a constitution that abolished slavery using the familiar language of equality. Noting "that all men are born equally free and independent, and have certain natural, inherent and unalienable rights," Vermont constitutionalists set the stage for slavery's demise. "[N]o male person, born in this country, or brought from over sea," the Vermont Constitution stated with finality, "ought to be beholden by law to serve any person, as a servant, slave or apprentice, after he arrives to the age of twenty-one Years, nor female, in like manner, after she arrives to the age of eighteen years, unless they are bound by their own consent." A similar reading of the New Hampshire Constitution had a like effect on slavery in that state. As in Massachusetts, slavery survived in Vermont and New Hampshire, for masters, even in the most marginal slaveholding communities, surrendered their valuable property with great reluctance. But it slowly weakened, so that by century's end few slaves remained in northern New England.[19]

ELSEWHERE IN the North, attempts to abolish slavery met stiffer resistance, as the ideals of the Revolution challenged the material benefits slavery provided to slaveholders and their allies. The confrontation between idealism and materialism became tangled as slaveholders drew their defense from the very ideology that stoked opposition to slavery. Revolutionary notions of liberty and equality adopted in state constitutions and elsewhere emphasized the right to acquire, hold, and protect property as an essential attribute of liberty. Virginia's Bill of Rights explicitly stated that "the enjoyment of life and liberty" rested upon "the means of acquiring and possessing property." In Massachusetts, New Hampshire, and other states, the founding documents did the same.[20] In 1789, the newly ratified federal Constitution added—even more strongly—its own guarantees of the sanctity of property, extending the slaveholders' reach into the free states, and limiting the legal and eventually the political grounds on which slavery could be contested. Slaveholders—eager to protect the benefits they derived from slave ownership—argued that human property was no different from any other and that, by law, property could not be expropriated without compensation. Giving practical support to the slaveholders' rights, the new federal Constitution provided slaveholders with disproportionate representation in the House of Representatives and the Electoral College, protected slave property though the Fugitive Slave clause, and allowed the importation of slaves from Africa for at least another twenty years.[21] The stark contest between the right to hold property and the right to be free yielded a signal victory for slavery.

The effects of the new protection that slavery received were evident in the struggle against slavery south of Massachusetts, where the sanctity of property rights and the essential role of slave labor shaped the debates over abolition. Nearly every proposal for slavery's eradication incorporated some form of compensation for slaveowners. Since neither the national nor the state governments evinced the slightest interest in assuming the burden of compensating slaveowners, slaves themselves—or, as it turned out, their children—would fund their own freedom through their labor.[22]

Black people and their allies, hampered by the weight of the slaveowners' rights and the need for slave labor, could only proceed under the assumption that freedom must arrive incrementally. They would not be freed immediately, and their children would gain their liberty only after years of service to their mother's owner or after years of what one historian has called "indeterminate status of non-contractual uncompensated servitude."[23] Even with these concessions, the possibility of emancipation met a storm of opposition, as slavery's friends articulated a host of arguments in favor of chattel bondage. They evoked slavery's long pedigree and universal presence, finding justification for property-in-man in the Bible and other ancient texts. They charged that people of African descent were "scarcely competent of freedom," emphasizing the social disorder and economic dislocations that would certainly accompany emancipation. Most importantly, they began to construct what would be the central trope of the proslavery argument: the figure of the happy slave, whose incapacity and dependency not only reflected his or her innate inferiority but also justified the role of the white master.[24]

Buoyed by the fierce opposition to black freedom, slaveholders attacked the heart of the antislavery argument, belittling the notion of universal equality and denying the possibility of a world devoid of slaves. As one New York opponent of emancipation put it, because black people were "extremely dependent, extremely ignorant, extremely indigent, and fiercely barbarous," they could never participate as equals in the American republic. The diverse circumstances and experiences of whites and blacks made equality a chimera, more a product of misplaced hopes than a clear-eyed appreciation of reality. A correspondent to a New York newspaper ridiculed the notion of turning a "sheep hairy African negro into a spirited noble, and generous American freeman!" Writing in the Philadelphia press, an apologist noted that some of slavery's opponents were "prejudiced against perpetual servitude from the maxim that . . . all mankind are born alike free. Oh flattering language!" he mused, "but not true" and hardly self-evident. Others followed with predictable lampoons that mocked the dialect and intellect of black people.[25]

And so it went. Every statement of equality was dismissed with searing denials that drew immutable differences between black and white people. When a writer calling himself "Gracchus" observed in the *New York Packet,* "All men have an *unalienable* right to liberty. But persons of a black colour are evidently *no men,*" he was swiftly rebuked and reminded that the absence of racial egalitarianism would destroy "Roman-like ideas of liberty." Others also found "Roman-like" liberty unpalatable. The seats in "our Senate and Assembly, General Quacco here, Col. Mingo there," would manifest "the shame we should most inevitably incur from mixture of complexion and their participation in our government." By the beginning of the nineteenth century, white abolitionists conceded that "many remained under the erroneous notion that blacks are a class of being not merely inferior to, but absolutely a different species from the whites . . . intended, by nature, only for the degradations and sufferings of slavery"—that they were, as Gracchus believed, "*no men.*"[26]

White abolitionists struggled against the mean, prejudice-laden assault, but their own ideas about black people also weighed heavily on the struggle for universal liberty. They denounced notions of the innate inferiority of black people derived from Jefferson's musings and so easily embraced by those who likewise saw "hairy Africans" taking their place in American state houses. But they believed those who had experienced slavery would need training—training that might extend for generations—in order to enjoy republicanism. The environmentalism that provided the intellectual bedrock of white antislavery at once promoted the movement for slavery's demise and, at the same time, compromised it.[27]

While the debate over freedom and race continued uninterrupted in every Northern state, perhaps it was only appropriate that the matter of equality—the central issue in the struggle over slavery—was first joined in Pennsylvania, the birthplace of Jefferson's Declaration. In 1776, soon after the Continental Congress affirmed its commitment to independence, Pennsylvanians turned to the matter of abolishing slavery. Building upon the work of a generation of Quaker abolitionists, the mobilization of the growing free black population, and the assertion in their own newly minted state constitution that "all men were born equally free and independent," Pennsylvania radicals rushed to make their state the first to end what they called a most odious "violation of the rights of mankind." Knowing that they would face considerable opposition, they tempered their eagerness for primacy by projecting the eventual expiration of slavery into an ever-receding future. In the initial draft of Pennsylvania's emancipation law, the status of those currently enslaved was left unchanged. The children of the enslaved would be freed, but they would be required to serve as indentured servants until age eighteen if they were men and until twenty-one if they were women. When the opponents of emancipation challenged even that cautious proposal, the friends of freedom quickly yielded amending the draft: the number of years the children of slaves would spend in servitude was increased to twenty-eight.[28]

In 1780, when the Pennsylvania legislature enacted abolition, the new law provided only for the liberation of those born after March first of that year, the date designated for freedom's arrival. Masters retained ownership of slaves born before the law went into effect, while children born to enslaved mothers after March first would be indentured to their mother's owner for terms of twenty-eight years. Slavery would eventually expire in the state of Pennsylvania, but—according to one

calculation—some men and women could be held in bondage until the middle of the next century.[29]

In the remaining Northern states, where slavery was even more deeply entrenched—particularly in the largest ports and the richest agricultural regions—freedom was even slower to arrive. Emancipation eventually prevailed, but not until 1784 in Rhode Island and Connecticut, 1799 in New York, and 1804 in New Jersey. Moreover, everywhere freedom arrived according to the post-nati formula of the Pennsylvania law, a stricture that delayed emancipation for decades, sometimes generations, recognized property-in-man, confirmed the idea that freedom had to be purchased, shifted the cost of freedom to black people, and, in some places, provided direct compensation to slaveowners.

New Jersey set a benchmark for the attenuation of freedom. It provided for the freedom of the children of slaves born after July 4, 1804; then it delayed the arrival of freedom for women until the age of twenty-one and for men until the age of twenty-five. Finally, in its 1846 constitution, the state declared them "lifelong apprentices."

Elsewhere the law was no guide to the reality of slavery. Although New York ended slavery with great fanfare in 1827, ten years later David Ruggles, founder of the city's Committee of Vigilance, declared: "It is a very prevalent error [to think] that there are no slaves in this state."[30] Also lost in the process was the idealism accompanying the expansion of freedom that had played such a large role in the passage of the 1780 Pennsylvania law. Illuminations and parades had greeted the arrival of freedom in Pennsylvania, yet four years later Connecticut emancipation was, as one historian has said, "utterly pragmatic; there was nothing idealistic or visionary about it."[31]

Still, the Northern commitment to emancipation was a signal moment in the nation's—indeed, the world's—history. The post-nati laws eliminated the natural increase of indigenous slaves as a source of bonded labor. For the new American republic, slavery would no longer be a continental institution. Emancipation under the law, no matter how compromised and delayed, deepened the North's commitment to free labor, beginning the process by which Northern states set themselves apart from the region where slavery continued to flourish. The distinction between North and South, free and slave states, gained new weight. While the sobering reality was that the new legislation freed not a single living slave, and that the final end to chattel bondage would have to wait decades, or in some places generations, the prospect of eventual freedom nonetheless transformed the expectations of whites and blacks, slaveholders and slaves. For black men and women trapped in bondage, it meant that freedom was a live possibility.[32]

THE EMANCIPATION that freed no one moved the struggle onto new ground. As the defenders of slavery feared, the passage of the emancipation laws, no matter how compromised, subverted slavery. Black people carried themselves with a new bearing. As their children shed the label of slave, they could envision a different future for their people, if not for themselves. With slavery's demise in the offing, they took the lead and pressured their owners to grant them freedom in advance of the legal requirement. Slaveholders, also aware of impending emancipation, agreed to negotiate an early arrival of freedom, though the cost to black people would be substantial.[33]

Rather than concede the possibility of freedom, many slaveholders hardened their opposition.[34] For them, the promise of freedom in the long run changed nothing in the short run, and they maintained old practices under a new name. These owners initiated a stubborn rearguard action, selling their slaves for the highest price they could get. Others plotted the repeal of the offending legislation. When that failed, some simply ignored the new laws and dared black people to assume the status of free men and women, maintaining the old regime with naked force. Angered by events which put them on the defensive, some masters turned sadistic, abusing their slaves with the most vicious of punishments. If black men and women dared to defend themselves, slaveholders—according to one black man—turned on them with "unheard of barbarity, for daring to take advantage (as we have done) of the law made in our favor."[35]

Black people who occupied the liminal status of being neither free nor slave—that is, those entitled to freedom in the future but still ensnared in "indeterminate status of noncontractual uncompensated servitude"—faced the greatest danger. Since most were children, slaveowners conspired to deny them knowledge of their eventual freedom, fraud-

ulently altering their ages on legal documents to
lengthen their term of servitude. Charging some
petty violation of those terms, masters went to court
to stretch the years in servitude, extending bondage
from childhood into the slaves' most productive
years. Indeterminate uncompensated servitude became more like chattel bondage, particularly as
the number of white people entering into servitude
declined. Masters frequently played a double game,
promising to accelerate the date of manumission if
their slaves paid an additional sum or guaranteed
exemplary service for a term; then they would re-
fuse to honor the bargain and would sell the slaves
to some distant place. Since Northern states invested little or nothing to enforce the new emancipation laws, former slaves—particularly children—
were always at a disadvantage.[36]

Such subterfuge typified the endless chicanery
slaveholders employed to maintain the old regime
in the shadow of the new. The deceptions to circumvent or thwart the emancipation laws played out in
endless variety. Unscrupulous masters denied essential knowledge to children born after the passage of
the post-nati statutes, refusing to inform them they

were free. Other slaveowners, for whom black people remained a marketable commodity, trafficked prospective freed people across state lines, sending them to places where slavery remained legal. With the rising price of slaves providing an incentive to sell black people, illegal sales rose to new heights.[37] Following the 1780 emancipation, slaveholding Pennsylvanians shipped would-be freedmen to New York; after 1799, New Yorkers sent them to New Jersey; after 1804, New Jerseyans transferred them to Delaware or Maryland—all trying to offset their impending financial losses.

As long as out-of-state sales remained legal, kidnappers had a cover to continue their operations on a massive scale. Reports of boats loaded with black people could regularly be found in the press. Most Northern states eventually prohibited selling prospective freed people out of state, slowing the trade-in-man. However, New Jersey lawmakers left the door open, perhaps more interested in ridding the state of slaves than in freeing them. The sale of slaves continued across New Jersey's borders.[38] Other slaveholders transported pregnant women to places where slavery was still legal, so the children would be born slaves. The practice became so common that Pennsylvania lawmakers ruled against it. That proscription hardly limited the masters' ability to disrupt the emancipation. Holding enslaved children hostage, they forced free parents to sign long-term contracts with scant compensation in order to continue living with their own children. Although the precise number of black people promised freedom under various legislation, court orders, and individual pledges in the North but sold into slavery in the South will never be known, they may well have totaled more than half of all those who had been promised their liberty.[39]

The growing trade in black people attracted others to the business. Cases of false imprisonment, illegal sales, and kidnapping became all too common. Some masters acted with stealth, sending the soon-to-be freed on errands from which they would never return. Others acted with force, bludgeoning their victims, often aided by thugs hired just for that purpose. "The inhuman crime of kidnapping," declared the American Convention of Abolition Societies in 1801, "has increased to an alarming degree."[40]

Kidnappers in the free states and slave traders in the slave states conspired to spirit away hundreds, perhaps thousands of black men and women. Since they cared little about the age, sex, or status of their victims, they swept up men and women who had long enjoyed freedom, as well as those who had but recently gained their liberty. If the shadows of a lonely wharf or a deserted country lane or an isolated farmstead worked well enough for some kidnappers, others acted openly, seizing their victims on a busy street in the light of day, bringing them before a compliant magistrate, and shipping them south. Children playing in the streets while their parents were at work made particularly easy targets. Some kidnappers brazenly broke into the homes of black people, assaulted them, and then carried off the children before the eyes of their horrified parents. Sometimes they seized entire families.[41]

By the second decade of the nineteenth century, kidnappers displayed little shame about what had become simply another business, carried on openly with few checks. In 1817, William Nelson, a professional kidnapper with long experience in the trade, arrived in Philadelphia undeterred by his prior arrest and conviction in Delaware. He had seized a free black woman and sold her to a slave trader in Maryland. She had escaped and the local sheriff had brought Nelson to justice, at least briefly. The kidnapper had been publicly whipped and cropped, meaning that his ears had been cut off, and then they had been nailed to the pillory—none of which had discouraged him from resuming his business at the first opportunity. After arriving in Philadelphia, he met with associates in the suburb of Southwark, where he received a warrant for the arrest of three alleged slaves currently living in the district of North Liberties. The three slaves—a black woman and her two sons, who were twenty-two and sixteen—resided with the woman's husband, James Smith, and all claimed to be free. Nonetheless, Nelson, the magistrate, and another well-armed confederate proceeded to North Liberties, gained entry to the Smiths' house through a subterfuge, and seized the woman and her children. When her husband "boldly asserted himself" to save his family, Nelson drew a pistol and threatened to blow Smith's brains out. Meanwhile, Nelson's confederate struck the elder son with "a short bludgeon, or loaded mace," leaving him unconscious and bloody. Nelson then dragged his captives through the streets to the office of the Southwark magistrates, where a man named Dawson, yet another confederate, swore they were slaves. Nelson had assumed no one would speak in favor of the captive blacks in this distant jurisdiction, but the Smiths' neighbors and friends had followed them and contradicted Dawson's testimony. A writ of habeas corpus was obtained. Rather than being sent off with Nelson, Mrs. Smith and her children were jailed and, when they came before the Supreme Court, released.[42]

Nelson walked off, presumably frustrated but still undeterred. He soon gained another warrant, this one to seize a certain "Sam, slave" on the pretense that he had a stolen watch. Dawson testified that Sam was a slave, and the nasty work of kidnapping continued, although this episode likewise ended happily when Sam was recaptured and eventually released.[43]

That such "outrages were committed upon a family of free people, in Philadelphia, and on the Sabbath day!" scandalized respectable white Northerners, horrified at the enslavement of men and women who presumably were living as free people in a free country.[44] Northern legislatures enacted new laws barring the sale of black people out of state and raised the penalties for kidnapping, but rampant corruption stymied enforcement.[45] Long supportive of the rights of slaveholders, who were often neighbors and friends, local magistrates looked the other way as masters and their accomplices did their dirty work. The 1793 federal Fugitive Slave Act removed the stigma of illegality and enabled kidnappers to act with impunity, empowering local magistrates to issue warrants for the "removal" of any black person charged with being a fugitive from labor. According to the law, no proof had to be offered other than the accuser's word, which was good enough to send the alleged fugitive into slavery.[46] Even as kidnapping became rampant, some slaveowners found ways of achieving their ends within the law, as they turned chattel into apprentices or indentured servants. Legal emancipation was only the beginning of the battle for freedom in the North.

Seeing promised freedom slip out of reach, the enslaved resisted attempts to be deprived of what they believed to be rightly theirs and their descendants'. In countless ways they made it clear that they would no longer brook bondage, challenging the various subterfuges that owners used to delay emancipation, confronting them directly and becoming authors of their own freedom. Half-measures and compromises of the post-nati system no longer sufficed.

Black men and women refused to suffer the delays mandated by the gradualist laws and extended by the slaveowners' deceptions. Now that freedom was a real possibility, negotiations took on a greater sense of urgency, as each side labored to come to a resolution. Inevitably the deliberations were tense and difficult, characterized by unspoken threats and wishful promises made on an uneven playing field of the slaveholders' power and the slaves' subordination. As the contenders traded threats and promises, black people realized that their masters still enjoyed a monopoly of force backed by the authority of the state, and slaveholders came to acknowledge that state-mandated freedom was in the offing. Black people, for their part, might threaten to malinger or might promise good service for a defined term in exchange for freedom at an agreed-upon date, but they knew they could be sold beyond the reach of the emancipation laws. Slaveholders, for their part, could make threats—they could wield the lash or put their chattel up for sale—but they were aware that their slaves might flee.[47] On such unstable and unpromising ground, black people sought to exit slavery.

IN THEIR DIFFICULT negotiations, black people found allies among the members of the increasingly active white abolitionist societies, who assumed responsibility for enforcing the emancipation laws—a task that might otherwise fall to the state. The reconstituted Philadelphia-based Society for Promoting the Abolition of Slavery (1784), the newly organized New York Manumission Society (1785), and the Connecticut Society for the Promotion of Freedom (1790)—along with other groups formed in Rhode Island, Delaware, Maryland, Virginia, New Jersey, and western parts of Pennsylvania—lent respectability to the movement and provided material resources for the slaves' struggle.

The antislavery societies and their affiliates offered elite lawyers to represent black people in court. From a deep knowledge of abolitionist legislation—some of which they had authored— they employed legal technicalities to expand the avenues to freedom. In Pennsylvania, to cite but one example, they scoured the state's records for slaveowners who had failed to register their slaves as required by law, and they hauled them into court, forcing them to surrender their human property. Members of the societies also served as surrogates, sitting at the table during delicate negotiations between slaves and their owners, and then monitoring the compliance with the agreement that emerged. Their voice amplified and strengthened that of the slaves in the court of public opinion, as they lobbied for universal freedom in the press and other venues that black people rarely reached. Their unquestioned patriotism and gentility provided a cloak of respectability for a cause that most whites disparaged.[48]

At a time when many—perhaps most—white Americans doubted black people's capacity for citizenship, white abolitionists generally stood by the principles of equality and held firm to an optimistic vision of a multiracial republic. The emancipation laws neither denied citizenship to African Americans nor barred them from voting if they met the qualification of being a property owner; that obstacle would come later. To be sure, white emancipationists maintained that the long years of bondage would have to be countered by long years of education and moral uplift (and they established schools for black children to meet that goal), but eventually blacks and whites would enjoy the equal freedom promised by the Declaration. Alexander Hamilton—a slave-holder, like many other members of the New York Manumission Society—noted that black people's "natural faculties are probably as good as ours" and that "the contempt we have been taught to entertain for the blacks, makes us fancy many things that are founded neither in reason nor experience." Still, white abolitionists were slow to act on their beliefs; they tolerated slaveholding among their members and excluded African Americans from the antislavery societies. Their emphasis on the need to prepare black people for freedom—hence their gradualism—fed doubts about the ability of black people to cope with the rigors of freedom. That members of the abolitionist societies proved to be the slaves' best friends only confirmed the weakness of the slaves' position.[49]

Of necessity, leadership of the struggle for universal liberty fell to African Americans, slave and free, who were steadily acquiring knowledge of their rights and how to defend them in a post-emancipation era. While the high-toned members of abolitionist societies worked carefully within the confines of the law, black people had little use for its niceties and for the abolitionists' counsel of "patience and forbearance," their preachy moralism, and what one scholar has called their "overbearing paternalism."[50] Black leaders gladly exchanged deference for the material and ideological support of the abolitionist societies from which they themselves were excluded. They appreciated the abolitionists' assault on prejudice, but their long years in bondage had left them with little tolerance for the slow unfolding of the law in which many of the white emancipationists were invested. In 1800, some of these tensions exploded when free blacks in Pennsylvania offered to pay a special tax to bring an end to slavery. The proposal irked white emancipationists, who considered this a tacit legitimation of slavery, as well as an obstacle to their own efforts at abolition. Black leaders seemed to care less about the formal legal recognition of slavery—whose reality they knew well enough—than about speeding slavery's demise. But they could do nothing to mitigate the opposition of their longtime allies, who scuttled their proposal even after it passed the lower house of the Pennsylvania legislature. Their failure only increased their desire to act independently.[51]

This new assertiveness was apparent throughout black society, as frustration mounted with the slow pace of slavery's demise in the North and the rapid expansion of slavery in the South. At every turn, black people demanded immediate abolition, and when it arrived they celebrated with speeches and parades. Unwilling to wait for the legal end of slavery, black men and women—particularly young men—simply seized their freedom, or, in a particularly apt phrase, "stole themselves." Their success, bought at the price of enormous risk, allowed the sharp increase in runaways that began during the Revolution to continue into the years following American independence. The growing number of free blacks not only camouflaged fugitives, but also actively aided them by providing information, forged passes, new clothes, places to hide, and of course the inspiring example that a black person could be free. Such assistance elevated even further the chances of success. With increased frequency, slave masters advertising for the return of fugitives warned that their runaways "will pretend to be free." The fact that there were many repeat offenders convinced some slaveholders that slavery was no longer viable.[52]

WITH SLAVES stealing themselves and slaveholders dragging black people back into bondage, the struggle over slavery devolved into direct confrontation. A New Jersey fugitive, who had previously contracted to buy his freedom but found his owner had nonetheless tried to sell him, denied his owner's right to put him on the market. He publicly pronounced that his owner had "no legal right to any such Negro Man, nor pretensions to claim myself." As conflict intensified, the violence inherent in slavery became ever more manifest. In one case, a New York slave turned on his mistress and beat her before taking his leave.[53]

The battle lines sometimes grew deadly. Determined to reassert their control even in slavery's death throes, slaveholders turned to the familiar offices of the law to enforce their authority. But often they took action themselves, employing the fist and the lash to assert their mastership. Black people were cautious about answering in kind, at least openly: the ordinarily lethargic legal system gained remarkable speed when they took up arms, even in self-defense. Yet, as slaveholders feared, enslaved black people became increasingly assertive, striking back at those who would deny their freedom. A series of trials of black women who poisoned—or attempted to poison—their owners filled white New Yorkers with dread, revealing how slaves might retaliate. So, too, did the fires that mysteriously ravaged cities in the Northeast during the 1790s. Though the authorities never identified the culprits, black arsonists were widely suspected.[54]

During the last years of the eighteenth century, the fears—real and imagined—that black men and women would seize their own freedom took on new meaning when the slaves in Saint-Domingue, on the west end of the island of Hispaniola, did just that. By the time Toussaint L'Ouverture deserted his Spanish patrons and assumed the leadership of an army of former slaves, hardly any Americans—white or black, free or slave—doubted the possibility that their world might be turned upside down. Black people on the island had not only freed themselves, but were in the process of establishing their own republic. As émigrés of all colors flooded into the United States, the stories of the violent end of slavery in Saint-Domingue remade the debate over emancipation. While the revolt stiffened the resistance of many whites to abolition, it made black people all the more determined to seize the moment.[55]

The new activism adopted various forms. In 1801, one Madame Volunbrun, a slaveowning refugee from the great rebellion on Saint-Domingue who had taken up residence in New York City, prepared to transfer her slaves from eventual freedom in New York to the certainty of slavery in Virginia. The New York Manumission Society moved to block her exit, claiming that her "slaves" had been freed by the French emancipation of 1794. As the society took its case against Volunbrun to court, black men and women took to the streets. "Armed with cudgels," they surrounded Volunbrun's house, "crying out that they would set the house on fire and murder every white soul in it" if the black people were not released. Eventually the city guard dispersed the crowd and arrested the rioters. The incident sent many of the black activists to jail; it also probably induced the New York Manumission Society to drop the case and to retreat from any implication of support for black violence. Within a year, Volunbrun quietly transferred her "people" to the slave state of Maryland.[56] But others remained—a fact that showed how difficult it was to drive a stake through the heart of slavery. A decade after New York had ended slavery, David Ruggles remarked that many people mistakenly believed there were no slaves in the state.[57]

Such failures, the glacial pace of the movement toward freedom, and perhaps the compromised position of white abolitionists—many of whom continued to own slaves—encouraged black people to become ever more visible advocates of their own cause. As the number of free blacks grew, they formed their own organizations, creating the rudiments of a civil society that paralleled the white one from which they had been excluded. Churches and fraternal lodges provided the institutional backbone for the nascent black community, but the network of black organizations extended from schools to burial societies.

No matter what their function, these organizations all included the word "African" in their name, to emphasize the unity of black people. Together they pressed for universal emancipation.[58] Building on such challenges to slavery, free backs demanded the rights of citizens: the right to vote, to serve on and testify before juries, and to join the militia. Emancipation laws neither eliminated old colonial proscriptions nor added new ones, but black people found themselves barred when they tried to exercise their rights. Soon thereafter, proscriptive legislation appeared, founded on the belief that the experience of living as a slave handicapped black people permanently. The habits of slavery or the hand of the Almighty had left black people unprepared and perhaps forever unfit to assume the responsibilities of republican citizenship. Blacks countered and won some early battles. In 1783 Massachusetts gave property-owning black men the vote, and other states followed. But, for the most part, African Americans were denied full equality. White Americans were afraid that free black people would become a burden on society, and their fears overwhelmed hopes for equality.[59]

As THE DEBATE over the standing of black people grew, Thomas Jefferson—whose words had fueled the movement for universal liberty—again intervened. In 1788, his discourse on slavery and race, written six years earlier in his *Notes on the State of Virginia,* reached print and attained wide circulation in the United States.[60] Its effect was palpable: Jefferson wound up stoking the counterrevolution against his own egalitarian revolution.

Jefferson began by reiterating his opposition to slavery. Failure to end the iniquitous practice would have dire consequences, and he evoked an apocalyptic vision of a retributive God. "I tremble for my country when I reflect that God is just: that his justice cannot sleep for ever: that considering numbers, nature and natural means only, a revolution of the wheel of fortune, an exchange of situation, is among possible events: that it may become probable by supernatural interference! The Almighty," Jefferson added, "has no attribute which can take side with us in such a contest." But black and white could not coexist in freedom, for "nature, habit, opinion has drawn indelible lines of distinction between them." These distinctions reflected Jefferson's "suspicion" that "the blacks, whether originally a distinct race, or made distinct by time and circumstances, are inferior to the whites in the endowments both of body and mind." The "unfortunate difference of color, and perhaps of faculty," he concluded, "is a powerful obstacle to the emancipation of these people."[61]

Here it was: the full weight of the judgment of the author of the Declaration. Jefferson would repeat it again and again in private correspondence and public utterances. In time, it would become universally known. Freedom for African Americans was inevitable—"Nothing is more certainly written in the book of fate than that these people are to be free"—but white and black could not coexist in freedom: "Deep rooted prejudices entertained by the whites; ten thousand recollections, by the blacks, of the injuries they have sustained; new provocations; the real distinctions which nature has made; and many other circumstances, will divide into parties, and produce convulsions which will probably never end but in the extermination of the one or the other race." Black people—hopefully slaves but certainly free blacks—must be physically removed from the American republic. Black people, or at least free ones, were inassimilable aliens in white America. The American republic could never elicit their *amor patriae*. Jefferson would spend the rest of his life searching vainly for the proper "receptacle" for African Americans, and in the process would lay the groundwork for the construction of a white republic.[62]

Jefferson's remarks collectively accounted for only a few paragraphs in the more than two hundred pages of his *Notes on the State of Virginia,* but they informed all future discussions concerning slavery, the character of black people, and the relations of black and white in the republic he helped to found.[63] For the defenders of slavery, and even for some of its opponents, they quickly became the conventional wisdom, in part because of Jefferson's authority and perhaps also because they expressed views that were already widely shared by white Americans. They fed a growing counterrevolution against the egalitarianism that Jefferson purported to represent as the nation's foremost spokesman for democracy.[64]

If Jefferson's position in 1786 contradicted the beliefs he had espoused some ten years earlier, they nonetheless exerted a powerful and immediate effect on the fledgling United States, whose new constitution cemented the rights of slaveholders, provided a path for slavery's expansion, and established the basis upon which slaveholders would dominate the American government for nearly seventy years.[65] In 1790, at its first meeting under the newly formed government, Congress denied Africans the right to become naturalized citizens; soon thereafter, it denied them the right to serve in the militia and even to deliver the mail.[66] The extent of the retreat from the first principles at the very center of the national government became fully evident when that icon of the Revolution, the much-revered Benjamin Franklin, introduced one of three petitions from the Society for Promoting the Abolition of Slavery: they urged Congress "to loosen the bands of and promote the general enjoyment of the blessing of freedom." Concurrent with proposals to end the slave trade, the petition endorsed by Franklin began, as did all claims to universal freedom, with the assertion that "equal liberty was originally the portion and is still the birthright of all men." Although it made no request for specific legislation, it urged a full "restoration to liberty of those unhappy men."[67]

Some Northern congressmen welcomed the petitions and supported the expansion of the movement against slavery from the state to the national level. George Thatcher, an antislavery representative from the Maine District of Massachusetts, privately congratulated the petitioners for promoting "the glorious cause of general freedom until we see the whole of the human race equally partaking of its Blessings." But the debate only exposed the naïveté of those opposed to slavery, for Southern representatives to a man considered the matter settled. They even doubted that Congress had authority to debate the subject; if it did, they would defend slavery to the last. Northern congressmen were divided, and ill-prepared to address the subject. Some spoke against slavery, but a solid core of congressmen conceded the legitimacy of an established institution and countenanced its existence for the foreseeable future. Few expected slavery to wither away, since it had become a permanent fixture in American life. For most, slavery's abolition—whether understood as impolitic, impractical, or immoral—was simply beyond their imagination.[68]

Listening from the gallery, members of the antislavery society were doubtless prepared to hear Southern representatives warn the Northern abolitionists against "meddling in a business with which they had no concern." Doubtless they were not surprised to hear South Carolina's William Loughton Smith defend slavery as an institution whose pedigree dated to ancient times, and which was sanctioned by the Bible and other authoritative texts. But Smith's disavowal of universal equality—the bedrock principle of the American republic—on the floor of the United States Congress may have shocked Northern lawmakers, particularly when he cited Jefferson's comments as evidence "that negroes were by nature an inferior race of beings." Thatcher was stunned that anyone would attempt "to prove the lawfulness and good policy of slavery." Still, not a single Northern congressman demanded an immediate end to slavery or denounced Smith's characterization of black people or asserted the equality of black and white. Their indifference and inaction sanctioned slavery. With little support from the emerging free states and with the active opposition of representatives from the slave states, the petitions of the abolition society were easily dismissed. The tenor of the debate over slavery had changed radically. Once Americans had been outraged at the presence of slavery; now they were outraged at the challenge to slavery.[69]

The federal government's commitment to slavery echoed in the states, where the counterrevolution against emancipation proceeded apace. As Northern states ended slavery in regions where there were few slaves, Southern states strengthened slavery in regions where there were many.

With the North's abolition of slavery, emancipationists had turned to the states of the upper

South—Delaware, Maryland, and Virginia—as obvious sites to expand the terrain of freedom. A flowering of emancipationist sentiment encouraged them. "Whilst we are spilling our blood and exhausting our treasure in defense of our own liberty, it would not perhaps be amiss, to turn our eyes towards those of our fellow men who are now in bondage under us," wrote "A Friend of Liberty" in Williamsburg's *Virginia Gazette* in the spring of 1782. "We say, 'all men are equally entitled to liberty and the pursuit of happiness' but are we willing to grant this liberty to all men?"[70] Evangelicals, particularly the rapidly growing Baptist and Methodist denominations, joined with Quakers to press for universal freedom. To be sure, support for emancipation remained weak. But by focusing on the slaveholders' right to free their slaves, emancipationists secured the liberalization of manumission laws, along with wider latitude for freedom suits. As slaveholders freed their slaves and as juries ruled in freedom's favor, the free black population swelled, increasing from some 2,000 in 1782 to 20,000 in 1800.[71]

But in the last decade of the eighteenth century, slavery's defenders gained the upper hand, as opposition to the growth of the free black population—indeed, even to its presence—became stronger. Jefferson's now-famous ruminations on the innate inferiority of black people and the revolt in Saint-Domingue catalyzed the opposition to black freedom. Among white slaveholders, the number of manumissions declined, and masters who freed their slaves rarely did so because of a commitment to equality. The courts, once a possible source of freedom, became a bulwark of slavery, as new legislation prohibited hearsay testimony, delegitimized the slaves' knowledge of their family's history, raised the requirements for proof of free descent, and confined freedom suits to unfriendly venues. Serious consideration of emancipation became impossible.[72] When St. George Tucker, scion of one of Virginia's first families, presented his gradualist plan to end slavery, the state's General Assembly refused even to consider it, in some measure because of white Virginians' "general opinion of their [blacks'] mental inferiority, and an aversion to their corporal distinctions from us." The door to freedom had slammed shut.[73] In 1800, with the discovery of Gabriel's Conspiracy—a broad-ranging insurrectionist plot to seize the city of Richmond and begin the destruction of slavery—it was sealed.[74]

Manumission, the chief remaining avenue to freedom, became the particular object of slaveholders' ire. The friends of freedom defended it— ironically staking their claim on the masters' right to free their slaves. Liberal lawmakers repeatedly beat back attempts to restrict manumission, but their margin of victory shrank with each confrontation. By the beginning of the nineteenth century, nearly every session of the legislature drew closer to reversing the decades-old liberalized manumission policy. The slide toward restriction gained momentum as the defenders of slavery hit upon a mechanism that would both restrict manumissions and reduce the state's free black population. It required the newly freed slaves to leave the state soon after receiving their freedom. When the opposition again sounded the nation's commitment to equality, the restrictionists spit back: "[T]ell us not of principles. Those principles have been annihilated by the existence of slavery among us."[75]

DURING THE FIRST decades of the nineteenth century, Revolutionary principles, if not annihilated, were most certainly attenuated, and not just in Virginia. The advance of slavery outpaced the advance of freedom. Between 1800 and 1820, the number of free blacks more than doubled, increasing to 234,000, but the number of slaves ballooned from nearly 900,000 to more than 1.5 million.[76] Bearing the brunt of the collapse of egalitarianism were free people of color. Most of them were newly liberated slaves, but others had pedigrees in freedom that reached back to the seventeenth century. Since they were viewed by whites as congenitally indolent, criminal, and insurrectionary, their liberty had long been restricted; various colonies denied them the right to vote, sit on juries, testify in court, serve in the militia, and travel freely. But the colonial proscriptions were neither systematic nor complete. While most colonies denied black people the suffrage, others granted them the right to vote; while some excluded black men from the militia, others allowed them to serve; while some burdened black householders with additional taxes, others did not.

In the face of a growing free-black population, especially in the North and the upper South, lawmakers systematized those old proscriptions and added new ones. Free blacks became subject to special punishments—incarceration or the lash—for crimes for which white people might be merely fined.

In many places, they were required to carry a pass. Practices once openly accepted were now denied. Thus, black men and women who had once openly attended churches with whites found themselves barred under the false claim of "custom." Taken together, the new systematic legal and customary constraints made a mockery of the egalitarian ideas that drove the expansion of black freedom. They left no doubt that free black people were less than "free," as Americans understood the term. American society was governed as much by the distinction between black and white as by the distinction between slave and free. While the new racial animosities spurred the growth of African-American institutions—indeed, a massive renaissance in African-American life—they came as a crushing blow to men and women who expected that with freedom they would take their place as citizens of the Republic.[77]

The new racial regime spurred black people to press the case against slavery. Perhaps it was in desperation more than in hope that Gabriel, an enslaved Virginia carpenter, and his allies—well-versed in the history of the American Revolution, inspired by events in Saint-Domingue, and committed to the egalitarian principles of the revolutionary age—plotted to take the town of Richmond and begin the process of destroying slavery. When a rainstorm derailed their plan and sent the plotters to the gallows, Gabriel had only to compare himself to George Washington to justify his actions. Gabriel's Conspiracy was only one of several conspiracies, rumored plots, and an outright insurrection that echoed through the new republic as slavery began its massive expansion and the possibilities of universal freedom faded.[78]

From the broadest perspective of the new order, it appeared that black people had exchanged one set of constraints for another—as the line between slave and free was transmuted into the line between black and white. To be sure, legal freedom, however compromised, was different from slavery. In freedom, black people governed their own families, collected their own wages, and formed their own associations, but the new regime ensured that they would be impoverished pariahs, living on the margins of American society and excluded from the great promise of American life. For most white Americans, the degradation and marginality of black people only confirmed Jefferson's "suspicion" that black people were "inferior in mind and body." While most white Americans continued to hold that inferiority was the product of circumstances, a growing number subscribed to Jefferson's belief in natural or providential differences.

With the new racial ideologies, the possibilities of emancipation disappeared into an ever-distant future. Congress admitted Kentucky (1792), Tennessee (1796), Louisiana (1812), Mississippi (1817), and Alabama (1819) to the Union as slave states, and, after a brief period of indecision, allowed Louisiana to import African slaves, most through South Carolina, which had reopened the direct African trade. In 1808, Congress had closed American borders to the entry of African slaves, but had done little to enforce the ban. An internal or interstate slave trade expanded and supplanted the international one as the mechanism for supplying enslaved laborers to the new plantation region. Meanwhile, the federal government ensured slavery's expansion by removing Native Americans from the land planters coveted in the Southwest; it did so by enacting one-sided treaties or, when necessary, by using force. In 1811, federal troops defeated a massive slave rebellion in Louisiana. They stood ready to protect slaveholders from slavery's enemies, allowing it to enter the period of its greatest expansion.[79]

The movement against slavery shriveled. Embarrassed by their inability to eradicate the last remnants of slavery in the North and utterly defeated in their attempt to end slavery south of Pennsylvania, white emancipationists largely gave up the battle. They fought a heroic rearguard action against kidnapping and other abuses of black people in the North, but could go no further. Everywhere, the Jeffersonian notion of purging the country of black people and sending them to Africa gained support among white Americans, claiming it could remove the ugly stain of blackness and slavery. Black people at first flirted with the idea of returning to Africa and reviving their ancestral homeland. But by 1816, when the American Colonization Society became the standard bearer for the transit of black people to Africa, most black people had distanced themselves from the idea, particularly as white colonizationists gratuitously denigrated them as inassimilable aliens. Although some determined white opponents of slavery continued to embrace colonization as a viable emancipationist strategy—perhaps the only viable strategy, given the intractable nature of white racial prejudice—black men and women had dubbed the scheme a dangerous subterfuge that strengthened slavery, exiled free blacks, and squandered antislavery energies.

Opposing colonization with a vengeance, black people asserted their rightful place in their American homeland. While they welcomed help from their old friends in the manumission societies, they continued to rely upon their own movement against slavery within their churches, schools, and civic associations.[80] By the end of the second decade of the nineteenth century, the movement for universal freedom had returned to its post-Revolutionary origins. The most reliable supporters—and sometimes the only supporters—were black people, whose commitment to equality proved the surest weapon against slavery.

Bolstered by the great expansion of black freedom and the phalanx of African-American institutions, black people took up the leadership of the antislavery cause.

3

The Bloody Struggle Endures

SOME FIFTY YEARS after the founding of the Republic, the lines of battle over slavery had been drawn. Slavery's opponents had won some hard-earned victories. Slavery fell throughout the Spanish Americas and, after Britain abolished slavery in its colonies, throughout much of the Caribbean as well. The dismantling of slavery in the Northern states created an enclave of freedom that some would liken to a Brazilian quilombo—a republic of runaway slaves.[1] Although the North remained deeply enmeshed in the ever-expanding national slavery system, slavery no longer dominated the entire North American continent. On the west end of the island of Hispaniola, after a brutal rebellion, slaves had created their own free republic. Liberated from slavery's shackles, black people—most of them former slaves—and their white allies joined to create an antislavery constituency that reached across the Atlantic, assaulting notions of hereditary aristocracy and racially defined hierarchies. They wove their increasingly sophisticated arguments against slavery into a coherent ideology, countering the slaveowners' age-old defense of chattel bondage. This, in turn, put the slaveholding class on the defensive and provided the foundation for a direct assault on slavery's Southern heartland.

But while the opponents of slavery had won some critical battles, they were losing the war. The friends of freedom were not always the friends of equality, and black people found their newly won liberty weighed down with many constraints. While the successful rebellion in Saint-Domingue mobilized antislavery sentiment, the violence that accompanied the birth of the Haitian Republic frightened many of slavery's opponents, chilling abolitionist sentiment. In the American South, the close of the transatlantic slave trade, rather than marking a singular defeat for the slaveocracy, dissolved many of the regional differences among slaveholders. It created a new unity, eviscerating the indigenous white opponents of slavery and inaugurating a Second

Middle Passage. Henceforth, slavery's growth would be the product of natural increase rather than importation. Employing the levers of constitutional privilege and partisan politics, slaveholders and their allies then translated regional power into national dominance, which allowed them to control the presidency, the national legislature, and the highest courts. Not surprisingly, the federal government did the slaveholders' bidding: its agents recaptured fugitive slaves, ignored the proscription on the transatlantic slave trade, and facilitated the massive westward expansion of slavery. By 1820, the number of enslaved black people had risen to over 1.5 million, more than triple that of the Revolutionary era. Emboldened by slavery's new vitality and protected by the Constitution, slave masters fortified their defense, imbuing it with a new stridency. Among slavery's defenders, some ceased apologizing for property-in-man and instead boasted of the advantages of slave labor as a way of organizing production and ordering society.[2]

The opponents of slavery enjoyed none of these strengths. Unlike the slaveocracy, they were divided not merely in strategy and tactics, but in their ultimate goal. While many white Northerners had a visceral disdain for slavery, other interests trumped their distaste. When the issue of slavery arose, there always seemed to be some other concerns—matters involving trade, internal improvements, or fiscal policy—that took precedence, relegating slavery to the margins. On those occasions when Northern representatives prepared to challenge slavery, some more attractive end inevitably hove into view and muted their voices. As white Northerners increasingly identified their region with the expansion of wage labor and celebrated its economic and moral superiority over forced labor, their engagement with the issue of slavery waned. Perhaps their collective conscience had been soothed by the demise of slavery in the North, freeing them from the taint of slavery. They no longer pressed their representatives to attack slavery; slavery was no longer their problem.[3] Reflecting the views of their constituency, Northern politicians shied away from a direct critique of chattel bondage, even as their region's swelling population gave them a majority in the House of Representatives. They welcomed a division between Northern and Southern states and the separate spheres in which free and slave labor might expand according to some rough climatological division. The notion that white men could not or would not work in a subtropical environment gained general acceptance in the North, much as it did in the South. The principle left little room to challenge slavery. As a result, opposition to slavery was sporadic and ineffectual. Surrendering the question of slavery to slaveholders allowed the masters to shape the issue to their own liking.

Of the white opposition to slavery, much was rooted in contempt for slaveholders and their perceived aristocratic pretensions and haughty ways. It had little to do with the slaves themselves and with the effects of slavery on black people. White Northerners had little sympathy for the plight of black people, and their fear and distrust of slaves as impoverished dependents was passed on to those who gained legal freedom. By confining the North's small free black population to second-class citizenship, white Northerners eroded their own moral authority respecting slavery. When confronted with the question of how they might deal with a mass of black slaves in their midst, white Northerners spouted platitudes or admitted frankly that they did not know. White Southerners—especially slaveholders—were quick to appreciate the advantage those empty replies provided. Such vacuous responses revealed that racism knew no sectional boundaries. In truth, the vast majority of white Northerners could no more imagine black people as their equals than could white Southerners. Shared racial beliefs hampered their ability to speak out against slavery, and diminished the power of their arguments when they did. Northern racism strengthened the slaveholders' hand. The masters enjoyed nothing better than turning the critiques of Southern slavery back upon their critics.[4]

However compromised and hypocritical, the ideas that drove Northerners to abolish slavery were not without force. The sectional divisions that emerged during the second war with Britain, between 1812 and 1815, particularly over the additional congressional representation the Constitution had awarded the slave states, gave the issue of slavery increased visibility. While the earlier admission of Kentucky, Tennessee, and Louisiana as slave states confirmed Southern understandings that slavery had a permanent place in American life, Northern opposition grew when Mississippi and Alabama applied for statehood following the War of 1812.[5] Then, in

1819, when the Territory of Missouri petitioned for full membership in the Union as a slave state, the simmering Northern resentment at slavery's expansion boiled over.

James Tallmadge, Jr., a maverick Republican representative from upstate New York, demanded that as a condition for statehood, the Territory of Missouri begin the process of ending slavery in accord with the gradualist, post-nati formula employed in the North. His proposal found vocal support among Northern representatives, who saw a last chance to eradicate the sin of slavery. "If Congress failed to act," one Northern congressman predicted, slavery would "strike its roots so deep in the soil that it can never be removed." But Southern congressmen— led by the Speaker of the House, Henry Clay— countered quickly with, if anything, more vehemence, making it clear they were united in their commitment to slavery. The raucous disputes that followed, known as the Missouri Debates, lasted through two congressional sessions and shook the Republic to its very essence, eventually setting the antislavery movement on a new path.[6]

Not surprisingly, the debates quickly focused on the Declaration and on its contested meaning. Tallmadge warned that the failure to restrict slavery's expansion would debase the nation's first principles and jeopardize the Republic's very reason for being. While some Northern representatives pressed the case for the Declaration's universality and its relevance to the slaves, white Southerners made it clear that such arguments were nothing short of criminal "for asserting the natural rights of these people." As the debates grew more heated, Southern congressmen accused Northerners of inciting an insurrection "which all the waters of the occasion cannot put out, which season of blood can only extinguish."[7]

Tallmadge stood his ground. "If a dissolution of the Union must take place, let it be so! If civil war, which the gentlemen so much threaten, must come, I can only say, let it come!" Tallmadge was willing to live with the bloody results of restrictions if his principles—and the nation's—could be maintained. At first a Northern majority sided with Tallmadge, and so, it seemed, did Northern opinion. But as in the 1790 congressional debate over the petition from the Society for Promoting the Abolition of Slavery, Northern representatives—preoccupied with matters of commerce and taxes—received only limited home-state pressure to address the question of slavery. Meanwhile, a united slaveholding constituency backed the phalanx of white Southern representatives, who were eager to demonstrate their support for slavery. In the end, "doughfaces"— white Northerners who were soft on slavery—in the House of Representatives and the Senate surrendered to the Southern insistence that limitations on slavery's growth would mean disunion. Few were willing to follow Tallmadge into a bloody civil war.[8]

Tallmadge's initial proposal met defeat, but the debate continued when delegates to Missouri's constitutional convention prohibited the entry of free blacks into the state. Many people thought this measure violated the Constitution's guarantee that the citizens of each individual state would enjoy the "privileges and immunities of the citizens of the several states." As the debate shifted from the question of slavery to the rights of black citizens and even the possibility of black citizenship, the matter struck at the heart of the commitment to equality. Southern congressmen flatly denied that African Americans could ever be citizens. South Carolina's ageless C. C. Pinckney, who had also attended the 1787 Constitutional Convention, assured all that when the

Constitution had been ratified "there did not then exist such a thing in the Union as a black or colored citizen, nor could I then have conceived it possible." He doubted that currently "one does exist." Northern congressmen silently conceded the case, having little interest in connecting equality to black freedom, although the attitude toward black citizenship—with respect to such things as suffrage, judicial and militia service, court testimony—differed from state to state. Black people, who listened intently to the debates from the capitol gallery and followed them in the press, were obviously disappointed at the decoupling of freedom and citizenship, although they could not have been surprised.

The Missouri Debates touched on every aspect of the question of slavery and race, revealing the full range of white sentiment on both matters. Northern congressmen held a clear majority in the House of Representatives and were equal to their Southern counterparts in the Senate. But in the end, even those representatives sympathetic to the antislavery cause muffled their voices, whether in deference to party unity, out of respect for the web of economic ties that linked Southern planters to Northern merchants and manufacturers, or from acceptance of the hardening racial divisions in both the North and the South. The divisions within Northern ranks contrasted sharply with the unity of Southern representatives, who may have differed on how they would defend slavery but stood as one in support of chattel bondage. Slavery and white supremacy again carried the day.

While the debate generated much heat—including dire predictions of national dismemberment, such as Jefferson's famous "fire bell in the night" that would portend "the [death] knell of the Union"—the resulting "Missouri Compromise" changed nothing of the essentials. Congress accepted Missouri as a slave state and conceded, in a mass of obfuscatory verbiage, the limitations on black citizenship. The simultaneous entry of Maine into the Union merely kept parity between free and slave state representation in the Senate. Likewise, the prohibition of slavery in the territories north of Missouri's southern border—the other element of the compromise—did little to change the spheres of freedom and slavery as most white Americans understood them.

By any account, the opponents of slavery had been routed. At the end of the second decade of the nineteenth century, slaveowners were not only continuing their westward expansion across the rich alluvial lands of the Southwest, but also, through a series of subterfuges, were eroding the prohibition of slavery in the Northwest. If the egalitarian idealism of the Revolution had cracked open the door to freedom's expansion, the Missouri Debates slammed it shut. For all but the most ignorant or naïve, the hope that slavery would eventually wither away had been crushed.

WITH THE FAILURE of the Missouri Debates to advance the cause of universal freedom and the demoralization of slavery's opponents, the antislavery movement once again faded from national politics and returned to the African churches, mutual-aid societies, and civic associations that had emerged with the post-Revolutionary growth of black freedom. Subjected to discriminatory regulations, denied a multitude of legal rights, and excluded from white organizations, free black people expanded the organizations in which they could get married, educate their children, worship their god, and bury their dead. In general, their numbers, their variety of activities, and their degree of visibility were greater in the cities than in the countryside, and greater in the North than in the South. In Philadelphia, Baltimore, New York, and other eastern cities, African Baptist and Methodist churches predominated. African Masonic lodges were most numerous in Boston and its New England satellites, while much of the associational activity took the form of Catholic sodalities in New Orleans and other Gulf ports.

Although these organizations assumed different forms in different places, their leadership wove them together, creating overlapping and interlocking networks that amplified their voices to give them a national reach. "Committees of Correspondence" shared ideas and aspirations, establishing a national outlook built upon recognition of the emergence of a new racism that excluded black people from electoral politics, and that forced them to speak for themselves rather than defer to white patrons. African churches and associations did not mediate their concerns through a network of white notables. Instead, black men and women—educated and articulate—spoke from the pulpit and the press and addressed the immediate concerns of black people, challenging disfranchisement, denouncing the absence of equal protection and equal access in the public sphere, and countering the dangers of kidnapping. These men and women became the voice of black people, free and slave, and the civil society they created became the leading edge of the struggle against slavery and for racial equality.[9]

Operating in the shadow of white opponents of slavery and reluctant to offend their patrons, blacks nonetheless desired—in the words of Samuel Cornish and John Russwurm, editors and publishers of *Freedom's Journal,* the first black newspaper—"to plead our own cause."[10] Black leaders continued to have their differences; but unlike their white allies, they did not fret about the dilemmas posed by large-scale emancipation or the need for partisan unity, issues that were of great concern to white opponents of slavery. Matters of tariffs, internal improvements, and banking policy did not trump their opposition to slavery or their desire to create a racially egalitarian community. For them, slavery was not merely a symbol of savagery and inhumanity; it *was* savagery and inhumanity. In short, the abolition of slavery stood first in the priorities of black people and their organizations, as did the matter of equal rights. The latter's importance grew as Northern lawmakers—many of them friendly to slavery—hacked away at the rights free blacks equated with citizenship: the right to sit on juries, the right to serve in the militia, and, most important, the right to vote. For black men and women, the questions of abolition and racial equality were one. The countless sermons, speeches, petitions, letters, pamphlets, and eventually newspapers that emanated from their meetings and conventions restored the Declaration and the biblical injunctions of equality—rarely heard in the Missouri Debates—to a central place in the movement for universal freedom.

As black people took control of the antislavery effort, it assumed a new form—less deferential, less gradualist and more direct, more strident, more confrontational—in a word, more militant. It relied less on alliances with white abolitionists and more on grassroots organizing in African-American communities, with their network of churches, lodges, and associations. Everywhere, the movement to abolish slavery was joined to the movement for racial equality. The movement for universal liberty now had a new shape.[11]

NOWHERE DID the differences between the black and white opponents of slavery appear more starkly than in the contentious struggle over the issue of colonization. The country had long been debating a scheme to remove black people from the United States and repatriate them in Africa, as a means of encouraging manumission by slaveholders and perhaps eventual emancipation under the law. By the 1820s, this plan was several decades old. Thomas Jefferson had first championed it in the aftermath of Gabriel's Conspiracy, and other like-minded men had seized upon Jefferson's proposal. In 1816, they had institutionalized it with the formation of the American Colonization Society. Many opponents of slavery embraced the idea, as a way to circumvent the seemingly implacable white opposition to even the most cautious proposal for post-nati emancipation south of Pennsylvania. Initially, black people, too, considered it the basis for an alliance: the colonizationists' promotion of emancipation and their interest in Africa buttressed blacks' own nationalist desire to bring the benefits of republicanism, capitalism, and Christianity to their ancestral land.[12]

But by the 1820s, if not earlier, the colonizationists had alienated black people. Their Jeffersonian belief that a multiracial republic was impossible compromised their abolitionist claims. In presenting the case for repatriation to Africa—or removal to almost anyplace—they disparaged black people, characterizing them as "notoriously ignorant, degraded and miserable, mentally diseased, broken spirited, acted upon by no motive to honourable exertions." Rather than free the slaves, many colonizationists wanted only to purge the nation of free blacks; some openly promoted removal as a means to secure slave property and eliminate the example that black people could be free. While colonizationists spoke of the voluntary migration of slaves and free blacks to their homeland, black people could imagine how the derogatory depiction of African-American life as criminal, parasitic, and subversive, along with the exclusion of blacks from the Colonization Society's leadership, could eventually lead to forcible deportation and banishment. This would, in effect, be a reversal of the slave trade that had dragged their ancestors across the Atlantic, with all the pain of broken families, dismantled communities, and devastated lives.[13]

Responding to the colonizationists' portrait of a broken, alienated, dispirited community whose character was corrupt and whose purposes were subversive, black leaders celebrated their American nationality, boasting of their role in securing American independence. They conceded that poverty and ignorance afflicted their communities, but observed the growing wealth and education of black Northerners. Although support for colonization could still be found within the black community, it was diminishing, as the vast majority turned against the scheme.[14]

Following the Missouri Debates, two men—Denmark Vesey and David Walker—came to epitomize, though hardly typify, the new style of antislavery activism that had emerged from the black community during the first decades of the nineteenth century. They connected North and South, free and slave, as they forged links between the urban free people of color who saw their rights obliterated by growing racism and the mass of slaves whose families and communities were being demolished by the Second Great Migration and the Cotton Revolution.

Men of the world, Vesey and Walker were well-traveled free tradesmen. They had read widely, schooling themselves in an autodidactic tradition that had become common among workingmen during the nineteenth century. Both had a direct knowledge of slavery and had felt the force of white racism. Inspired by the success of the Haitian revolutionaries and fearful of the changes unleashed by the explosive expansion of American slavery, they urged black people to take matters into their own hands, encouraging them to rise up, overthrow their masters, and create a social order based on the principles of the Declaration of Independence. While few black men and women openly embraced violent proscription, their actions and their words revealed a growing willingness to confront slaveholding directly.

Vesey, the older of the two, had been born a slave in the Caribbean a decade prior to the American Revolution. Working for a slave trader, he sailed the Atlantic and was carried by his owner to Charleston, where in 1800 he won a lottery and used his winnings to purchase his freedom. A skilled carpenter, Vesey found a place in the Charleston community somewhere between the African-born slaves, who labored at the city's docks and manufactories, and the sophisticated, often light-skinned creole free people of color whose shops lined the city's streets. Through the force of his personality, the extent of his connections, and the depth of his knowledge, he gained a reputation as a man of independence who spurned even the most trifling acknowledgment of white superiority. The sight of a black man yielding the sidewalk to allow a white man to pass was enough to earn Vesey's rebuke. He observed that "all men were born equal, and that he was surprised that anyone would degrade himself by such conduct; that he would never cringe to the whites." When he received the answer, "We are slaves," he would "sarcastically and indignantly reply, 'You deserve to remain slaves.'"[15]

Vesey's angry refusal to accept white domination was well known in Charleston. He participated in the failed attempt to establish an independent black church linked with Richard Allen's Philadelphia-based African Methodist denomination. He followed, with disgust, the Missouri Debates. The inability of black people to gain a modicum of independence or take even a small step toward freedom may have driven him to organize a wide-ranging conspiracy to overthrow slavery, or may have made him an easy target for an ambitious city attorney eager to promote himself as someone who could protect the white community from black revolutionaries. In either case, Vesey's arrest, trial, conviction, and execution as an insurrectionist made him an exemplar of antislavery activism to a generation of black men and women growing up in the shadow of slavery's expansion.

David Walker may have been one of those young men inspired by Vesey's martyrdom. Walker had been born free in North Carolina just a few years prior to Vesey's chance liberation at the turn of the century. As a young man, he may have been in Charleston during the organization, discovery, and perhaps the trial and execution of Vesey and his fellow conspirators. From that coincidence or his own experience, Walker's ideas—and his deep anger—followed those of the older revolutionary. Walker migrated north to Boston, where he quickly became a central figure in the city's black community, a member of the African Methodist Church, an initiate in the Prince Hall African Masonry Lodge, and a subscription agent for *Freedom's Journal,* published in New York City. In 1828, he gave the keynote speech at the first meeting of the Massachusetts General Colored Association. His address denounced the pathetic state of disorganization of black life, excoriating "those who delighted in our degradation" and who "glory in keeping us ignorant and miserable." Walker called for the creation of an institution "to unite the colored population, so far, through the United states . . . forming societies, opening, extending, and keeping up correspondence." The speech was printed in *Freedom's Journal* and read far beyond New York.[16]

One year later, Walker published his *Appeal to the Colored Citizens of the World,* in which he explained the sources of African Americans' misery and offered a solution to their impoverishment and degradation.[17] Filled with classical allusions and providential judgments, along with numerous references to world history, the *Appeal* set out the ideas that had been developing within the largely self-taught black intellectual class, where notions of evangelical Protestantism mixed with ideas of classical republicanism. It relentlessly assailed American slavery as barbaric and inhumane, denounced the indignities that free blacks faced, and pointed to the contradictions between the treatment blacks endured and the professed ideals of the American people and their leaders. Walker had little trouble cutting the knot of contradictions. He called for massive slave resistance of the sort that sent icy shock waves through the planter class and distressed not a few white Northerners.

But the *Appeal* was equally hard on black people, free and slaves. Like Vesey, Walker had little patience with black men and women who bowed to white superiority. He condemned their servility, maintaining they were complicit in their own oppression. Black people bore responsibility for their condition: "We Coloured People of these United States are the most wretched, degraded, and abject set of beings that ever lived since the world began." He urged them to confront their oppressors and, if the confrontation turned violent, "kill or be killed." "Now, I ask you," Walker concluded, "had you not rather be killed than to be a slave to a tyrant, who takes the life of your mother, wife, and dear little children?"[18]

But Walker directed his heaviest guns at white Americans for their presumption of racial supremacy. His utter contempt for the self-serving and hypocritical reading of the nation's founding charters by the leaders of the Republic became the distinguishing mark of the *Appeal*. Taking particular aim at Jefferson, "one of the great characters as ever lived among the whites," Walker quickly disposed of Jefferson's theories of black inferiority and his plan to colonize African Americans, ridiculing Jefferson's apostasy from his own principles, along with the hypocritical, self-serving Christianity of the white Founders. Instead, Walker held tight to the great truth of the Declaration and the biblical prophecies, and claimed that black people were the true inheritors of the Revolution. While pressing black men and women to turn upon the hypocrites and pretenders and create a new world of freedom and equality, he also held out the olive branch of peace. His conditions: whites must relent, give up slavery, and embrace their own principles of equality.[19]

Like Vesey's conspiracy, Walker's *Appeal* frightened slaveholders and many other whites, even as they dismissed it as incoherent ranting. But it quickly earned Walker the allegiance of generations of people of color. It was reprinted in the North, and was carried to the South sewn into the garments of sailors. The *Appeal* captured the rage of an enslaved people and became an underground classic within the black community. For a rising generation of black abolitionists, it was required reading. Walker's central message was that the "full glory and happiness" of the "coloured people under Heaven shall never be fully consummated but with the entire *emancipation of your enslaved brethren all over the world.*" While white opponents of slavery dithered over colonization, the new generation of African Americans—urged on by Walker— denounced colonization and demanded a direct confrontation with the slaveholding enemy. Like Walker, they claimed to be Sons of the Revolution and marched under the banner of the Declaration of Independence.[20]

THE DEMAND FOR an immediate end to slavery and the creation of a slave-free world informed the emancipationist drive of black people in the aftermath of the Missouri Debates, even as most white opponents of slavery remained ensnared by the colonizationist vision of a white America. It was this understanding of slavery's end that black abolitionists passed on to a new generation of antislavery whites, most notably William Lloyd Garrison. The story of how black Baltimoreans converted a willful, morally righteous young man to immediate abolitionism is one of the set pieces of abolitionist historiography. Garrison, who journeyed to Baltimore as an apprentice to the Quaker journalist

Benjamin Lundy, initially shared Lundy's sentiment that—given the deep racism of white
Americans—colonization provided the only practical route to emancipation. Jacob Greener and
William Watkins, two of Baltimore's most prominent black schoolteachers and representatives of
the new generation of black leaders, instructed
Garrison on colonization's faulty logic and the
racism underlying it.[21] The pupil soon surpassed
his teachers. Garrison—rejecting the teachings of
Lundy and other antislavery colonizationists—
went on to write perhaps the most devastating critique of colonization. Unlike the earlier generation
of white abolitionists, he saw no need for black
people to undergo a long apprenticeship before
they could enjoy all the rights of white Americans.
Freedom would bequeath equality. Garrison's
practical egalitarianism won him the respect of
free black activists, and they came to view him as
an ally. Greener and Watkins, drawing upon their
ties with black leaders in Northern communities,
put Garrison in touch with free black leaders along
the Atlantic coast, men and women who would
eventually become the intellectual and financial
backbone of Garrison's abolitionist journal *The*

Liberator—and *The Liberator* became, in many ways, their journal. Of the approximately four hundred first-year subscribers, Garrison counted three hundred to be black.[22]

Garrison rose to be a central figure in the movement against slavery, animating the ideas that had long informed abolitionist thought in the black community. His opposition to slavery—like that of the black people, free and slave, for whom he spoke—stemmed from the Declaration and from the biblical promise of political and spiritual equality. It demanded nothing less than the creation of a multiracial republic. He and his allies repeatedly compared the guarantees in the Declaration ("We hold these Truths to be SELF EVIDENT—that All men are created Equal") with the enslavement of "millions in our midst, because they have sable skin . . . and crisped hair," returning to the theme of hypocrisy in their call for an immediate end to slavery.[23]

The advent of Garrisonianism represented the transformation of black society, which, in turn, was a response to the new racism—with disfranchisment in New York and Pennsylvania—that had all but denied a place for black people in American politics. The leaders of the new generation, which was represented at first by David Walker, included such figures as David Ruggles, Frederick Douglass, Henry Highland Garnet, Maria Stewart, and Alexander Crummell. Their forte was not placating white patrons or mediating between black and white, but mobilizing black people through their own autonomous institutions.

Garrison, in short, channeled David Walker—denouncing colonization, demanding that all "people *ought* and *must* be FREE," warning of apocalyptic violence unless white Americans mended their ways, and accepting nothing short of an egalitarian world.[24] Like Vesey and Walker, Garrison spoke to black people North and South, although the structure of black life differed greatly in the two regions. In embracing the central tenets of black abolitionism, as they had been developed in black churches and schools, Garrison and his followers faced the same violent retribution that had long been meted out to black people. White abolitionists were mobbed, beaten, and, in at least one case, murdered. An angry crowd nearly lynched Garrison on the streets of Boston.[25]

The kidnappings that had followed emancipation early in the nineteenth century became endemic during the years that followed, as Northern slave masters teamed with Southern slave dealers to send prospective free persons—as well as many black men and women who had long enjoyed freedom—into lifetimes of bondage. The owners and dealers were aided by state and municipal laws passed under pressure from Southern slaveholders and enforced by complaisant local and states magistrates. Pennsylvania and New York sanctioned writs of habeas corpus for slave catchers, permitting them to secure the arrest of any alleged fugitive. Armed with the writs, slave catchers could bring any black men or women before the court under spurious purposes, have them jailed, and ship them south to a lifetime in slavery.[26] For many free blacks, the situation was dire indeed, as old agreements failed to protect and new laws left them increasingly vulnerable. "We have no protection in the law," declared David Ruggles in 1836, "because the legislators withhold justice. We must no longer depend on the interposition of the Manumission or Anti-Slavery Societies."[27]

Kidnapping became a growth industry. Motivated by the rising price of slaves, a legion of slave catchers and manstealers—known as "blackbirders"—

congregated in the cities of the North. New York City became, in the words of one abolitionist, a "slaveholders' hunting ground." Everywhere, kidnapping schemes sent black men and women, often free or having been promised freedom, to a lifetime of labor on the plantations of the Deep South. Across the Hudson River, in New Jersey, one Jacob Van Wickle, a judge in county court, partnered with Charles Morgan, a Louisiana slaveholder, to establish a regular route that shipped prospective freedpeople from New Jersey to the cotton fields of the Deep South. Van Wickle ignored the statute stipulating that freedpeople could not be removed from the state without their consent. He and Morgan brazenly marched coffles of slaves to the docks of Perth Amboy, then loaded them onto ships that carried them up the Mississippi. The result, as New Jersey senator James Wilson declared, was that "many free persons, or who were soon to be free, had been consigned to slavery for life." Although vilified as a "soul driver" by some, Van Wickle was never convicted of any crime and his honorific title of "Judge" suggests his continued good standing in his community.[28]

The ongoing slave trade was just one element of the reign of terror that accompanied the revival of abolition.[29] It seemed to bear no relation to Garrison's pacifist principles or to the more formal program of moral suasion embraced by some abolitionists. Garrison and his white supporters became the target of vicious mobs, who taunted and assaulted them. But black people bore the brunt of the wave of terror. In one city after another, they found African-American neighborhoods invaded, churches and schools trashed, homes sacked, and residents pummeled. The sources and nature of the violence varied from place to place. In 1829, there was a systematic pogrom to cleanse Cincinnati of its black population; in 1833, street gangs dismantled Philadelphia's growing network of black institutions; in 1834, there was a challenge to racial mixing in New York City; and a year later there was a similar confrontation in Detroit. Others followed with increasing regularity as mobs of white thugs, often orchestrated by men of wealth and standing, targeted the most successful black entrepreneurs, the leading black activists, and the most visible signs of economic prosperity and social respectability of black people: churches, Masonic lodges, schools, insurance companies, publishing houses, and mercantile establishments.[30]

The new assaults did not signal a reduction of the older attacks. Kidnapping continued apace, as the price of slaves skyrocketed with the expansion of Southern cotton and sugar production. An unholy alliance represented by Judge Van Wickle, Charles Morgan, and others—slaveholders, complicit officials, professional slave catchers, and occasionally black collaborators—what one black abolitionist called "Kidnapping Clubs," seemed to be everywhere. "No colored man is safe," asserted knowledgeable New Yorkers, as the clubs regularized the business of recapturing fugitive slaves and used the search for runaways as a pretext to seize any vulnerable black person, no matter what his or her status. The attempts to enslave free black men and women became more systematic, although, as before, children remained the most prominent targets. "The alarming *fact*," according to a declaration by New York's "Friends of Human Rights" in 1835, was "that any colored person within this State is liable to be arrested as a *fugitive from slavery* and put upon his defense to prove his freedom, and by that any such person thus arrested is denied the right of trial by jury, and therefore subject to a hurried trial, often without the aid of a friend or counselor." The all-but-inevitable guilty verdict ensured that the alleged fugitive would be consigned to lifelong slavery.[31]

THE INCREASINGLY open violence and the atmosphere of terror that prevailed did not long go unanswered. Garrisonian nonresistance was cold comfort to those who saw their communities invaded and their families and friends forcibly enslaved. Whatever its strategic and ideological value in the public debates, nonresistance had little purchase among the mass of black men and women. With increasing frequency, black men and women directly confronted the kidnappers and the police who abetted them; David Walker's advice to "kill or be killed" seemed less like the raving of an extremist and more like simple common sense.[32] An 1826 confrontation in New York City, typical of many others, revealed the emerging pattern. A number of black men and women were seized by slave catchers or kidnappers. The status of all of these individuals was subject to claims. The local black community was quick to distinguish free from slave, but cared little about the distinction, believing all had the right to freedom.

The slave catchers and kidnappers had their own designs, and a confrontation naturally occurred between the largely black crowd and the hardened men who earned their living capturing runaways. When the authorities intervened, the black bystanders followed the police to the courthouse, where they milled around, trading rumors and speculations. When it appeared that the fugitives— in this case, a family of Virginia slaves—would be sent to their alleged owner on the south side of the Potomac, the crowd erupted. Black men and women stormed the judicial hearing, attacking the police who guarded the proceedings and momentarily freeing the black family. The fugitives were eventually recaptured, but the confrontation revealed the increased willingness of black men and women to challenge the slaveholding enemy and the constituted authorities who stood with the masters.[33]

By creating safe houses for runaways, publicizing the presence of slave catchers, denouncing complicit officials, and unmasking traitors within the black population, New York's established black community gained a modicum of relief from kidnappers and established a safe harbor for fugitives. After a year of operation, the city's Committee of Vigilance, founded by David Ruggles, issued a report of some eighty pages declaring that it had saved some 330 people from slavery and listing scores of confrontations. The following year, the committee rescued 600 black men, women, and children. "The pleas of crying soft and sparing never answered the purpose of reform, and never will," declared Ruggles.[34]

Vigilance committees sprouted quickly in the angry mixture of urban poverty and official racism in which black people lived. Like most antislavery organizations, they were fully integrated at the top, where prominent white opponents of slavery played a visible role. As with *The Liberator,* for which Garrison served as editor and to which black men and women made up most of the subscribers, the complexion of the members of the vigilance committees darkened as one descended through their ranks. Much the same was true of the Underground Railroad. Some activists—such as New York's Louis Napoleon, an illiterate porter who was later declared to be responsible for the successful escape of some 3,000 fugitives—worked closely with and sometimes ahead of the white and black leaders of the Vigilance Committee and the Underground Railroad in New York City. These organizations were known throughout the black community. Although traitors who would betray a fugitive could be found scattered through the black communities, more likely than not an unknown black man or woman would provide a trove of knowledge about the nearest safe house, a place that offered a warm meal, directions, and safe passage northward.

These black men and women, who earned their living pushing a broom and washing clothes for the white establishment, made up the crowds that blackbirders found so intimidating. One antislavery newspaper noted, assessing the role of white and black opponents of slavery, that white abolitionists were timid compared to the black crowds. "It may be doubted whether much would have been accomplished" had they tried to rescue a besieged fugitive.[35]

Ruggles's organization found imitators all over the North as vigilance committees sprang up everywhere, especially in towns and cities along borders with slave states. Even a small city like Harrisburg, Pennsylvania, with a population of only a few thousand, sheltered, by one count, 150 fugitives.

Together, black residents and the Vigilance Committee's efforts to protect the city's fugitive population were often enough to ward off slave catchers and kidnappers. But not always. In 1850, the entire black community of Harrisburg mobilized to prevent the seizure of three fugitives from Virginia, leaving a slaveholder bloodied and ten black men subject to arrest warrants. Eventually, several slaves made it to freedom, others did not, and the skirmishes continued for the next decade.[36]

The physical and often bloody confrontations went on despite the ideological arguments about the efficacy of violence that were taking place among leading abolitionists, black and white. The reality of the street was fast converting those leaders, who were shedding nonresistance along with the politics of deference.[37] Ruggles found an ally in a distinguished fellow New Yorker, the physician James McCune Smith, who had come to believe that "our white Brethren . . . recognize only the philosophy of force." Others—Henry Highland Garnet, Alexander Crummell, and even Frederick Douglass—sounded the same theme. Douglass asserted, "The only way to make the Fugitive Slave law a dead letter is to make half dozen or more dead kidnappers."[38]

But the vigilance committees had their hands full. "Scarcely a day passed without a new case," observed Ruggles, speaking of New York, and others reported the same. The fugitives' presence drew slave catchers and the usual complement of blackbirders. They were armed, vicious, and unafraid of the law, which was often complicit in their nefarious business. The "alarming fact," Ruggles continued, was that "any colored person within this state is liable to be arrested as a fugitive from slavery, and put upon his defense to prove his freedom, and that such person thus arrested is denied the right to a trial by jury." Kidnappers found it easy to confuse runaways with free blacks and to treat free blacks as if they were runaways. The result was an increasing number of confrontations.[39]

The undeclared but no-less-real war over slavery had a different dynamic in the slave South, where black people did not dare to organize vigilance societies in the open. But compared with groups in the North, clandestine networks in the South were just as effective in aiding fugitives, and the confrontations with slave catchers just as bloody. Only a small portion of the runaways—estimated at some 50,000 annually—aimed for freedom. Most were truants, eager to escape the harsh routine of slavery for a few days but with no substantial plans to seize their liberty. Of those who aimed to escape slavery permanently, many headed for the most inaccessible regions of the South—swamps and mountains— where they found refuge among established maroon colonies. But the life of a maroon was difficult, perhaps more difficult than life under slavery, making cities more desirable hideaways. There fugitives could camouflage themselves among the mélange of free blacks, hired slaves, and other black people who lived independently and enjoyed a degree of autonomy unimaginable on a plantation or farm. Urban officials established a mass of regulations— registering black workers and issuing badges—to control black people; still, numerous men and women gained their freedom in Southern cities, sometimes passing as free, establishing families, and even purchasing property.[40] But even the most secure fugitives—like free black people—lived on the edge. When their freedom was challenged, they did not surrender and meekly return to slavery, where brutal punishments awaited. Rather, they confronted masters, patrols, and slave catchers with guns, knives, and axes. The bloody battles that followed left a trail of wounded and dead, not all of them black.[41]

THE ONGOING urban warfare in the North and the South paled in comparison to the strife in the rural borderlands. Reaching from Delaware in the east through Maryland and northern Virginia, and along the Ohio River Valley into Kentucky, Ohio, Indiana, and Illinois, the region was characterized by small farms and workshops which employed a diverse labor force of slaves, hired enslaved workers, wage workers (black and white), indentured servants (many of them immigrants), and sharecroppers. Since neither slave nor free labor was dominant, workers and bosses bargained for the most advantageous arrangements, creating hybrids that sometimes made black and white workers competitors and companions. Some white employers became advocates of wage labor, while others favored slavery. The circumstances spurred fugitives and their friends to press for freedom and, at the same time, encouraged slaveholders and their allies to hold the line. Constant simmering conflict, punctuated by threats of sale southward and counter-threats of slave flight, left everyone in a state of "unpleasant apprehension" and prepared the ground for open warfare.[42]

In Maryland, on the slave side of the line, traders were dragging thousands of black men and women to the cotton plantations of the South. Slaveholders found themselves facing enslaved black men and women who were determined to resist and to prevent their families from being sent southward. Many slaves fled north, confronting their antagonists in the process. In 1822, a black man ambushed a slave trader carrying the man's family south, and "lodged the content of a musket" in his side. During the years to come, such solitary acts became, in the words of one historian, "a guerrilla war against slavery." Black men and women attempted to liberate relatives and friends; slaves took flight, battled former masters, found safe havens in the North, and then returned to liberate others. The cross-currents made for a war zone.[43]

Over the next twenty years, the conflict grew more violent. In 1845, when a Maryland sheriff confronted some ten fugitives near the Pennsylvania border, he found that the slaves, "armed with hatchets, clubs, and pistols"—like most runaways—

refused to be taken without a fight. When the battle ended, several white men and about half the fugitives "had been wounded and only one of the fugitives had been taken into custody."[44]

Such conflicts occurred regularly across the western end of the border between slavery and freedom. In Illinois, where all manner of chicanery breached the Northwest Ordinance's prohibition on slavery in the region, the struggle over slavery moved from the state house and the courthouse to open hostilities. In 1842, kidnappers led by one John Crenshaw seized Maria Adams and her extended family, some of whom were free and some of whom were indentured servants, and sold them all to Texas. This sale of free persons aroused the opponents of slavery, who tried to recover the Adams family and pressed a grand jury to indict Crenshaw and his gang. Unwilling to wait for the law to do its work, however, Maria's husband and her brothers, Charles and Nelson, assaulted Crenshaw and beat him severely. Soon after, Crenshaw's mill mysteriously burned to the ground. But black men's independent efforts to balance the scales of justice offended the whites who previously had been horrified at the kidnapping of Maria Adams and her family. Crenshaw's friends and sympathizers now had new leverage. The day Crenshaw's mill burned, his allies whipped an "unoffending old black man," sparking an explosion of violence in which white gangs terrorized the local black community. Soon afterward, a jury acquitted Crenshaw, while another convicted Charles and Nelson of arson. Crenshaw walked away free, Charles and Nelson went to prison, and Maria and her children remained in slavery. Black activism had a price.[45]

The situation in the borderlands encouraged slave masters to rise quickly to the defense of their human property and spurred black people to move with similar alacrity to seize their liberty, lest the Fugitive Slave Act close the door to freedom. While black people like the Adamses may have learned the limits of their power, those who labored shoulder-to-shoulder in the same fields or workshops might provide protection against kidnappers, even shield a runaway or provide information that could aid an escape to freedom. As one abolitionist observed about the struggle between black and white in the borderlands, "There is much in these cases to alarm the oppressor and encourage the advocates of the oppressed."[46]

The ongoing violence gained greater intensity—and greater visibility—with the passage of the Fugitive Slave Act in 1850. The new law reinvigorated the old 1793 act and made all Americans responsible for its enforcement. The federal treasury assumed the cost of slave catching. As before, the alleged fugitive had no right to a jury trial and no right to testify on his or her own behalf. The burden of proof was on the black captives, but they had no power to prove their freedom. In addition, they were now taken before federal commissioners—many of them Democratic appointees—who would be paid ten dollars for each black person returned to his or her owner, and half that amount for each fugitive who was not returned.[47]

The law touched all Americans: free and slave, slaveholders and abolitionists, Northerners and Southerners. It empowered and energized slaveholders, who understood the law as confirmation of their right to property-in-man, as well as providing practical ways in which they could protect that property. It mobilized the slaveholders' friends, an unsavory crew of slave catchers, kidnappers, and complicit law officers who found profit and satisfaction in the enslavement of black people.

The Fugitive Slave Act shocked black neighborhoods; no one was now safe from enslavement. Fugitives living as free in the North had special reason to fear, as anyone could be claimed as a slave under the new law and have his or her standing affirmed by an official of the federal government. Black people by the thousands scrambled for safe havens, whether in Canada, Mexico, the Caribbean, or Europe. Others lived in a state of constant anxiety. But the initial panic was followed by a sense of resolve, a collective realization that the new threat had to be met with an equal determination to protect freedom. Some slaves, perhaps desperate to seize a last opportunity for freedom before the Fugitive Slave Act closed off opportunities for escape, saw the need to act in haste. Vigilance committees and Underground Railroad stations, many of which were based in the small black border towns or so-called freedom villages that developed on the northern side of the Ohio River, could still make possible a successful escape.[48]

THE COLLECTIVE resistance to rendition and the willingness to purchase the freedom of those forcibly carried south helped to make the Fugitive Slave

Act increasingly unenforceable—but not unchallengeable, as the conflict became open warfare.[49] In Christiana, Pennsylvania, a confrontation at a small crossroads town exemplified the heightened level of violence caused by the Fugitive Slave Act, the willingness of black people to risk all for freedom, and the equal determination of slaveholders to secure the chains of bondage.[50]

By the middle years of the nineteenth century, slave flight had become common along the Maryland-Pennsylvania line. In the fall of 1849, it was assumed that four slaves who had fled from Edward Gorsuch's plantation located just north of Baltimore were following a well-trodden path. Nonetheless, like many slaveholders, Gorsuch was surprised by their desertion; he believed he had treated his slaves well, even to the extent of promising them freedom in the future. Still, he did nothing until the passage of the Fugitive Slave Act armed him with a new weapon—and perhaps a new determination—to secure their return.

By then, however, Gorsuch's former slaves had found a home near the village of Christiana in Lancaster County, where black men and women, many of them fugitives, worked as farm hands in a community led by one William Parker. Across a wide swath of Lancaster and neighboring Chester County, Parker had gained a reputation as the kidnappers' worst enemy. A former slave who had escaped in 1839, Parker early on had formed an association for self-defense, the rural equivalent of Ruggles's Vigilance Committee. With the support of a small group of white opponents of slavery, mostly Quakers and Methodists, Parker and his reputation kept most kidnappers at a distance.

Parker's presence did little to deter Gorsuch, who enjoyed not only the support of his son and other kinsmen but also the full weight of the United States government, in the persons of federal marshals from Philadelphia. He met the marshals in Philadelphia and together rode west toward Christiana to confront Parker and the fugitives. Upon their approach, Parker's wife sounded the alarm, and the black residents turned out en masse, filling the roads and fields around the Parker compound, determined to maintain their freedom and that of their newly arrived friends. When Gorsuch pressed the case, gunshots rang out and he fell, mortally wounded. The Gorsuch party, including the federal marshals, fled, and eventually so did the fugitives.

The former returned to Philadelphia and the latter disappeared into the web of vigilance committees and Underground Railroad stations, outdistancing a local posse and a contingent of United States Marines sent to track them down. Parker, too, headed north and, with the aid of Frederick Douglass, found refuge in Canada.

The death of Gorsuch and the ensuing manhunt, successful escapes, and trials attracted wide attention. A grand jury in Lancaster County indicted thirty-eight men on some 117 counts of treason. Prominent abolitionists such as Lucretia Mott and others raised money to support the defense, which was led by congressman Thaddeus Stevens. In the end, no one was convicted.

The bloody Christiana Affair suggested how the Fugitive Slave Act would aggravate the violent confrontations in the years to come, increasing their lethality, intensity, and visibility. And those encounters would occur in rapid succession, making it clear that black people would settle for nothing less than freedom and that freedom could be obtained only by violence. In 1851, an abolitionist crowd composed of delegates to a Liberty Party convention freed a runaway named William Henry, who had been living as Jerry McHenry in Syracuse, New York. Soon after that, slave catchers in Boston seized Shadrach Minkins, a fugitive from Virginia. When the judge refused to issue a writ of habeas corpus and instead remanded him to the local jail, the local vigilance committee broke into the jail and sent Minkins on his way to Canada. Such successes put Boston officials on high alert, and attempts to rescue fugitives Thomas Sims and Anthony Burns failed. Nonetheless, these attempted and successful renditions of fugitive slaves became signature events of the decade much as did the border war in Kansas, the caning of Charles Sumner, and John Brown's assault on the federal arsenal at Harper's Ferry.[51]

WHILE THE SUCCESSFUL—and failed—escapes seized national headlines and preoccupied the political classes, more and more black men and women were pulled into the vortex of efforts to abolish slavery and secure equal standing with white Americans. The violence that had been part of the struggle against slavery from the beginning moved ever closer to organized, state-supported conflict.[52]

Yet the possibilities of realizing that long-term goal of equality faded when, in 1857, Chief Justice

Roger Taney opened the entire country—including the North and the territories—to slavery and barred people of African descent from membership in the larger American political community. Capping his decision in *Dred Scott v. Sandford* with the chilling words that black people "had no rights a white man is bound to respect," Taney's decision left the long-stated claim of black people to equality in a shambles and their assertion of citizenship a fiasco. Taney had braced the foundation of white supremacy.[53]

Following Taney's decision, black activists held a series of meetings—some of which were formal conventions and others ad hoc gatherings—in which they took turns denouncing the *Dred Scott* verdict as a "foul and infamous lie, which neither black men nor white men are bound to respect." In Troy, New York, a convention of colored people which drew delegates from all over the state rehearsed the powerful counter-narratives they had developed during the post-Revolutionary years to assert their claim. They spoke of the Boston Massacre, the martyrdom of Crispus Attucks, and the Declaration of Independence, and highlighted the role of black soldiers in securing independence. Others carried the narrative into the nineteenth century, restating their role in securing and maintaining American independence during the War of 1812, denouncing colonization as a fraud, and denying that their *patria* could be any other country but the United States. These mainstays of African-American political rhetoric, along with the charges of hypocrisy against those white Americans who asserted the universality of equality for whites but not for blacks, had a long history in African-American life. "We are citizens of the State of New York, and consequently, of the United States," proclaimed a delegate to the New York convention. Hence, they should "enjoy all the rights and immunities of other citizens."[54]

Distinguishing many of these occasions was the presence of black men in arms, as the vigilance committees transformed themselves into militias. The Liberty Guard of Boston, the New Bedford Independent Blues, the Hannibal Guards of Brooklyn, the Attucks Blues of Cincinnati, and dozens of others took part in marches, displaying their skill with bayonets and performing maneuvers, making it clear they were prepared to fight for their rights.[55]

Other opponents of slavery joined the protests against Taney's opinion, but their criticisms rarely extended to offering black people a full place in

American life. Instead, drawing on notions associated with the Free Soil Party—which opposed the expansion of slavery into the Western territories—they emphasized how *Dred Scott* threatened the rights of white people, degrading their labor by identifying it with that of black people and slavery. Indeed, for many whites, the critique of *Dred Scott* became the occasion to add their voice to the racially exclusionist chorus. Once again, the voice of black people distinguished itself from that of white opponents of slavery.

Black people took the lead in attacking Taney's verdict against their right to a full place in the American community. They answered the question of what would replace slavery as they always had: with a ringing defense of equality as the central tenet of American nationality.[56] Those who had been at the heart of the struggle to end slavery remained there. And it was not long before the violence that had always been an intimate part of the near-century-long opposition to slavery manifested itself again, in a far greater conflagration—one that would finally secure the long-sought freedom.

Coda

Free at Last

THE CIVIL WAR changed nothing and everything. Black men and women, slave and free, remained in the vanguard of the movement for universal freedom, demanding immediate emancipation. As emancipation became the issue that could not be avoided, the status of the newly freed slaves rose to prominence. Once it became evident that black people would no longer be slaves, the question became what, precisely, their status would be. Within the American context, the Declaration of Independence's assertion of equality and the biblical injunction that all are equal in the sight of God afforded only one answer. Abolitionists pushed for the equality and independence promised in the nation's founding charters.[1]

Freedom came to most American slaves through force of arms. The mobilization of warring armies that transformed the war for union into a war for freedom ratcheted up the level of violence well beyond the seizure of a handful of fugitives or the snatching of black children off Northern streets. The Civil War marked the first systematic use of the weapons of modern warfare. More Americans would die in the Civil War than in all of the nation's conflicts combined. Among the casualties were tens of thousands of black soldiers and perhaps an even larger number of black civilians, most of them slaves. The process by which slaves gained their freedom was soaked in blood.

The defining characteristics of the war for freedom were identical to those of the long struggle for universal liberty that had begun with the post-Revolutionary emancipations. Black people took the lead in demanding slavery's end, although the locus of black activism moved from Northern free people of color to Southern slaves. Questions of equality quickly became central to the debate over the future of the former slaves.

Just as it had done in the decades before the war, slavery came apart in pieces. In August 1861, shortly before adjourning, Congress enacted what would be the first of two Confiscation Acts, making all property used in support of the rebellion "subject of prize and capture." The act's provisions revealed the growing importance of runaways, who were crowding into the Union army's lines and offering their labor in support of the federal cause. High on the list of property to be confiscated were slaves used to support the rebellion. The success of the First Confiscation Act encouraged congressional radicals to press emancipation's cause.[2]

Other pieces soon fell into place. During the following session, in March 1862, Congress added a special article of war prohibiting Union soldiers from returning fugitive slaves to their owners. Within a month, Lincoln signed legislation abolishing slavery in the District of Columbia.[3] Although the measure compensated slaveowners and provided for the colonization of former slaves, the new law constituted the first time the federal government had directly legislated the emancipation of any slave. Together, the legislative acts passed during 1862 formed the bedrock upon which slaves would stand firm and emancipation would eventually be built.[4]

African-American men and women poured into the Union camps, sometimes reciting the exact provisions of the new legislation that had provided for their freedom. Federal commanders welcomed the new arrivals, putting them to work on Union lines, and radical abolitionists cited their growing numbers as proof of their desire for freedom. But the status of the new arrivals, as defined under the 1861 law, begged for clarification. In July, Congress provided just that with the enactment of a Second Confiscation Act and, simultaneously, the Militia Act. The new legislation guaranteed that the slaves of disloyal masters would be "forever free of their servitude" and ordered that they "not be held as slaves again."[5] The Second Confiscation Act went far beyond the first, whose provisions had touched only those who were employed in Confederate service. Taken together with the Militia Act, the various measures enacted in the summer of 1862 brought the final emancipation closer.

As this chronology suggests, from the beginning of the war, the strongest advocates of universal freedom were the slaves themselves. Lacking political standing or public voice, and forbidden to acquire weapons of war, slaves nevertheless tossed aside the grand pronouncements of Lincoln and other Union leaders that the sectional conflict was only a war for national unity. They moved their own freedom—and that of their descendants—to the top of the national agenda. Steadily, as opportunities arose, slaves risked all for freedom. By abandoning their owners, crossing into Union lines, and offering their labor and their lives to the federal cause, slaves forced federal soldiers at the lowest level to recognize their importance to the Union's cause. That understanding traveled quickly up the chain of command, to the officers, to their civilian commanders, to elected officials in Congress, and to the presidential palace. In time, it became evident even to the most obtuse federal commanders that every slave who crossed into Union lines was a double gain: one subtracted from the Confederacy and one added to the Union. The slaves' resolute determination to secure their liberty converted many white Northern Americans—soldiers and civilians alike—to the view that the security of the Union depended upon the destruction of slavery. Eventually, this belief tipped in favor of freedom, even among Yankees who displayed little interest in the question of slavery and had no affection for black people.

The slaves were not without allies. Free blacks, particularly Northern ones who had a long history of antislavery activism, stood at their side. Most white abolitionists dismissed the official Republican doctrine that slavery should be respected and given constitutional protection where it existed. Instead, abolitionists, like the slaves, saw the war as an opportunity to demonstrate the immorality of chattel bondage and press for its extirpation. Rather than condemn slavery from the comfort of their drawing rooms, some radical opponents of slavery volunteered to fight slavery on its own terrain; they strapped on their haversacks and marched south as part of the Union army. But soldiering was young men's work, and sex, age, condition, and circumstance barred many from the federal army. Most abolitionists could only fume against slavery in petitions, editorials, and sermons. Although their campaign on behalf of universal freedom laid the foundation for congressional and then presidential action against slavery, the majority of abolitionists had but slender means of attacking slavery directly. Only the slaves had both the commitment and the opportunity to initiate a direct assault on slavery.

Some slaves did not even wait for the war to begin. In March 1861, before the first shots were fired at Fort Sumter, eight runaways presented themselves at Fort Pickens, a federal installation on the southern coast of Florida, "entertaining the idea"—in the words of the fort's commander—that federal forces "were placed here to protect them and grant them freedom." The fort's commander believed otherwise and delivered the slaves to the local sheriff, who returned them to their owners.[6] Although their mission failed, these eight fugitives were only the first to evince publicly a conviction that eventually became widespread in the slave population: the belief that the war was being fought to help them acquire their freedom.

In making the connection between the war and freedom, slaves also appreciated that a Union victory was imperative. They did what they could to secure it, throwing their full weight behind the federal cause, volunteering their services as teamsters, stable hands, and boatmen; butchers, bakers, and cooks; nurses, orderlies, and laundresses; blacksmiths, coopers, and carpenters; and, by the tens of thousands, as common laborers. Slaves "tabooed" those few in their community who shunned the effort. Hundreds of thousands of men and women would work for the Union, and more than 135,000 slave men would become Union soldiers. Even deep within the Confederacy, where escape to federal lines was nearly impossible, slaves did what they could to undermine the Southern war effort and strengthen the Union cause. With their loyalty, their labor, and their lives, slaves provided crucial muscle and blood to support the federal war effort. No one was more responsible for smashing the shackles of slavery than the slaves.[7]

Using the weapons they had, slaves drove the issue of emancipation to the top of the wartime agenda. They could not vote, pass laws, issue field orders, or promulgate great proclamations—that was the task of citizens, legislators, military officers, and presidents. Yet the actions of slaves made it possible and necessary for citizens, legislators, military officers, and the president to take action on the matter of emancipation. Slaves were not the only movers in the drama of emancipation, but their assertion of their rights and their willingness to die for them made them the prime movers in this final assault on slavery.

How they did so is nothing less than the story of emancipation.

AMONG THE SLAVES' first students were Union soldiers of the lowest rank. Arriving in the South with little direct knowledge of slavery and often contemptuous of black people, federal soldiers encountered slaves who were eager to test their owners' fulminations against Yankee abolitionists and black Republicans. Union soldiers soon found their camps inundated with slaves, often breathless, tattered, and bearing marks of abuse. The runaways faced sure punishment if captured; their flight to Union lines entailed substantial risk.

Still, some gained entry into federal lines, where they found work aplenty. Sometimes the slaves' labor cut to the heart of the soldiers' military mission, as when they imparted information about Confederate troop movements, assisted in the construction of federal fortifications, and guided Union troops through unfamiliar terrain. But just as often, slaves ingratiated themselves with federal soldiers in ways that had no particular military significance. They foraged for firewood, cooked food, cleaned campsites, and performed dozens of onerous tasks that otherwise would have fallen to the soldiers themselves.

Northern solders did not have to be Free Soilers, abolitionists, or even radical egalitarians to appreciate these valuable services. So they were dismayed to discover that they had violated orders by harboring the fugitives. They were even more upset when the men and women who cleaned their camps and cooked their food were dragged off to certain punishment by angry masters and mistresses. Indeed, even those soldiers who stoutly maintained that they were fighting solely for the Union bitterly resented being implicated in the punishment of men and women who had done nothing more than do good work in exchange for a blanket and a few morsels of food. "I don't care a damn for the darkies," declared one Midwestern volunteer in March 1862, "but I couldn't help to send a runaway nigger back. I'd be blamed if I could."[8] The "blame" many Union soldiers felt at being implicated in slavery was compounded by the outrage at the fact that the very same men and women they had returned to bondage were being mobilized by the Confederate enemy to fight against them. To Union soldiers, the folly of denying themselves resources that their enemy used freely—indeed, assisting their enemy in maintaining those resources—seemed senseless to the point of absurdity.

Further up the chain of command, federal officers were learning those same lessons. The protection and employment offered to fugitive slaves by individual soldiers created numerous conflicts between slaveholders and the Union army, embroiling officers in heated disputes whose resolution required considerable time and effort. Slaveholders, many of them brandishing Unionist credentials, demanded that federal troops return fugitives who had sought protection within their encampments. If regimental officers could not or would not comply, they blustered that they would appeal to connections reaching the highest levels in Washington. Generally, the bluster was just that. But often enough, officers would soon feel the weight of high authority upon them. Officers of the middle ranks bore not only the brunt of the soldiers' frustrations with federal policy, but also the sting of official rebuke. Made apologists for policies they believed contradicted personal experience and good sense, many field officers found themselves in the uncomfortable position of having to enforce regulations they disdained. They objected particularly to having to do the masters' dirty work, and they intensely disliked being demeaned before their troops. The high-handed demands of slaveholders turned many federal officers into the slaves' champions.

Pressure from the bottom pushed on those at the top. When federal policy toward fugitive slaves finally changed, in the summer of 1862, one could hear an almost audible sigh of relief from the Union officer corps. "The thing of guarding rebels' property has about 'played out,'" one officer remarked. "We have guarded their homes and property long enough. . . . The only way to put down this rebellion is to hurt the instigators and abettors of it. Slavery must be cleaned out."[9]

As pressure from the bottom pushed on the middle ranks of the Union military, so pressure from the middle ranks was felt at the top. Eventually, it reached the very top. In July 1862, just before informing his cabinet of his intention to announce a proclamation of emancipation—the so-called Preliminary Emancipation Proclamation—Lincoln was quizzed about what he thought was the best course. He responded rhetorically, in a letter laced with sarcasm: "Would you drop the war where it is? Or, would you prosecute it in future, with stalk squirts, charged with rose water?" Lincoln, of course, had no intension of doing either. "This government," he commented at the end of July 1862, "cannot much longer play a game in which it stakes all, and its enemy stakes nothing."[10] Henceforth, he would use all the weapons at hand, including that of the slaves. He not only freed them on January first, but he also invited slave men to enter the Union army.

The war had turned. Nothing more clearly marked the transformation of the war for union into a war for freedom than the appearance of black men in blue uniforms. Black Yankees served as the best recruiting agents, drawing thousands of slaves, reluctant to accept the leadership of a white man, into the federal forces. Once the enslaved men entered the black regiments—the United States Colored Troops—the process by which slaves became free men acquired momentum. The new recruits no longer wanted merely to escape their limited lives under slavery—they demanded the rights that accompanied freedom.

IN MARCH 1863, the struggle over the meaning of freedom emerged in both the military and civilian branches of the Lincoln administration. The most pressing issue was the status of black soldiers, who had been guaranteed equal treatment. Black men who entered the Union army had been granted one of the great attributes of citizens. Like Frederick

Douglass, many believed that all the rights of citizenship would flow naturally from the basic right of equality. "Once let the black man get upon his person the brass letters US, let him get an eagle on his button, and a musket on his shoulder, and bullets in his pocket," Douglass famously proclaimed, "there is no power on earth or under the earth which can deny that he has earned the right of citizenship in the United States."[11] There is a great deal of evidence that Douglass was correct. Military service, as one historian has noted, gave black soldiers "some sense of personal achievement, and a share in the nationalistic enthusiasm of the North." It advanced black men "toward the goal of real freedom."[12]

But what was "real freedom"? Whatever it meant, others were not as confident that the federal government was about to bestow it upon black soldiers. John A. Andrew, the antislavery governor of Massachusetts, like other abolitionists, implored Secretary of War Edwin M. Stanton to offer a guarantee of equal treatment, which Stanton, after some hesitation, eventually did. But the federal government violated virtually every such promise, and in so doing raised critical questions about the meaning of "real freedom."

No transgression of Stanton's pledge caused as much hardship or so blatantly insulted the dignity of black soldiers and their families as the policy of discriminatory pay. The general poverty of the black population made pay inequities an especially sensitive issue. Most black Northerners toiled as day laborers or domestic workers and owned little property. Probably many had never earned more than the thirteen dollars, plus clothing allowance, that the army offered white volunteers. The newly emancipated slaves were even more impoverished, since few escaped slavery with more than the clothes on their backs. Under such circumstances, black soldiers felt betrayed by the War Department's decision to pay them three dollars less per month than white soldiers, and to deduct an additional three dollars for clothing. The federal government's default on its pledge challenged the rights of black people as citizens at the very moment that military service, in the eyes of many, seemed to affirm racial equality. It was a stark reminder that racial prejudice pervaded Northern as well as Southern society. Black soldiers refused to accept pay inequality. They declined any pay until they received equal pay, despite the hardship this denial caused them and their families. At least one black soldier was court-martialed for his refusal. In the end, soldiers won equal pay—an important landmark in the long struggle for equality. But their struggle sharpened their realization that freedom was not to be given; it had to be taken.

Even as the War Department and its soldiers clashed over the matter of equality within Union ranks, the Lincoln administration acknowledged its own responsibilities to former slaves. In a practical way, these derived from the same questions; but in this case, the administration respected the status of black men and women who labored in the government's numerous fortifications, warehouses, landings, and hospitals, and in the contraband camps that housed their mothers, wives, children, and elders. Of course, these matters derived from exactly the same question that had been addressed in the fight for equal pay for black soldiers. Indeed, they harked back to the question raised by the liberation of the first slaves at the end of the eighteenth century. Although numerous individuals and organizations would address this matter throughout the war and the postwar period of Reconstruction, the range of the Lincoln administration's initial probe set the direction and scope of subsequent discussions of the wartime and postwar status of former slaves.

That status was affected by numerous circumstances, not the least of which was the war itself. New military technology—most especially the rifled musket and the lead bullet known as the Minié Ball—increased the accuracy of rifles many times over, with deadly results. It drove up mortality rates and made the Civil War the deadliest of all American conflicts to date. The most recent estimates of wartime deaths range from 752,000 to 851,000. These, of course, do not include those maimed and traumatized by the war.[13] Death struck disproportionately on black soldiers—and, one presumes, civilians—in other ways as well. Whereas nearly two white soldiers died of disease for every one who fell in battle or died of wounds, the ratio among black soldiers was roughly ten to one. Part of the imbalance—again reflecting back on civilian mortality and morbidity—was that many black recruits were ill-prepared for soldiering. Slavery had left them weak and susceptible to disease, which was rampant in the crowded, unsanitary camps and hospitals.[14] Like all wars, the Civil War was a killing machine, bringing to a head the violence that had long accompanied the process of emancipation.

In understanding the demise of slavery in the United States, the character of the wartime abolition differed little from that of the more than half-century of struggle for universal freedom that had preceded it; only the scope and size were new. As in the antebellum period, black people took the lead in demanding freedom. Once freedom had been obtained, they wrestled with their owners and with local, state, and federal authorities over the status of former slaves, employing, as points of debate, the Declaration of Independence and biblical injunctions for equality. To break the bonds of slavery required as much energy as had originally been needed to form those bonds—or perhaps even more. Emancipation was ever a violent process, even more violent in the 1860s than in the antebellum years.

The characteristics of antebellum and wartime emancipation were much the same. They differed according to time and place, as any historical phenomena do, but their long history can be understood as one piece.

Notes

Introduction

1. Lieut. Edward M. Stoeber to Brev. Major S. M. Taylor, 24 July 1865, S-5 1865, Registered Letter Received, ser. 2922, South Carolina Asst. Commissioner, Records of the Bureau of Refugees, Freedmen, and Abandoned Land, National Archives.

2. Ibid.

3. See, for example, Lerone Bennett, *Forced into Glory: Abraham Lincoln's White Dream* (Chicago, 2000); Richard Striner, *Father Abraham: Lincoln's Relentless Struggle to End Slavery* (New York, 2006).

4. Seymour Drescher and Pieter C. Emmer, eds., *Who Abolished Slavery? Slave Revolts and Abolitionism: A Debate with João Pedro Marques* (New York, 2010).

5. João Pedro Marques, "Slave Revolts and the Abolition of Slavery: An Overinterpretation," in Drescher and Emmer, eds., *Who Abolished Slavery*, 8, 13, 20.

6. Ibid., 37.

7. Ibid., 67, 194.

8. Ibid., 73, 191.

9. Roy P. Basler, ed., *The Collected Works of Abraham Lincoln,* 9 vols. (New Brunswick, NJ, 1953), 8:333.

1. The Near-Century-Long Demise of Slavery

1. Kate Masur, "A Filmmaker's Imagination, and a Historian's," *Chronicle of Higher Education,* 30 November 2014, blog; Louis P. Masur, "Lincoln at the Movies," *Chronicle Review,* 30 November 2012, B6–B8; Michael Vorenberg, "Spielberg's Lincoln: The Great Emancipator Returns," *Journal of the Civil War Era,* 3 (2013), 549–572; also *The Atlantic*'s roundtable on the film at http://www.theatlantic.com/entertainment/category/lincoln-roundtable/.

2. J. Douglas Deal, *Race and Class in Colonial Virginia: Indians, Englishmen, and Africans on the Eastern Shore of Virginia during the Seventeenth Century* (New York, 1993), 217–250; T. H. Breen and Stephen Innes, *"Myne Owne Ground": Race and Freedom in Virginia's Eastern Shore, 1640–1676* (New York, 1980), ch. 1.

3. Arthur Zilversmit, *The First Emancipation: The Abolition of Slavery in the North* (Chicago, 1967); Ira Berlin, *Slaves without Masters: The Free Negro in the Antebellum South* (New York, 1975), chs. 1–4.

4. T. Stephen Whitman, *The Price of Freedom: Slavery and Manumission in Baltimore and Early National Maryland* (Lexington, KY, 1997); Richard Dunn, "Black Society in the Chesapeake, 1776–1810," in Ira Berlin and

Ronald Hoffman, eds., *Slavery and Freedom in the Age of the American Revolution* (Charlottesville, VA, 1983), 49–82; Eva Sheppard Wolf, *Race and Liberty in the New Nation: Emancipation in Virginia from the Revolution to Nat Turner's Rebellion* (Baton Rouge, LA, 2006), 69–72, 112–115; Loren Schweninger, "Freedom Suits, African American Women, and the Genealogy of Slavery," *William and Mary Quarterly,* 71 (2014), 35–62, esp. 41–42.

5. Wolf, *Race and Liberty in the New Nation,* 63–64.

6. Alan Taylor, *The Internal Enemy: Slavery and the War in Virginia, 1772–1832* (New York, 2013), 441–442.

7. Sylviane A. Diouf, *Slavery's Exiles: The Story of the American Maroons* (New York, 2014).

8. The estimate, admittedly an informed guess, is by Eric Foner in *Gateway to Freedom: The Hidden History of the Underground Railroad* (New York, 2015), 4, drawing largely from secondary sources.

9. *Population of the United States in 1860* (Washington, DC, 1864), 598–605. Since many census takers also served in various capacities as law enforcement officials, free blacks had reason enough to avoid them. The official enumeration was thus a substantial undercount of free blacks.

10. Ira Berlin, Barbara J. Fields, Steven F. Miller, Joseph P. Reidy, and Leslie S. Rowland, *Slaves No More: Three Essays on Emancipation and the Civil War* (Cambridge, UK, 1992).

11. Foner, *Gateway to Freedom;* Fergus M. Bordewich, *Bound for Canaan: The Underground Railroad and the*

War for the Soul of America (New York, 2005), 225; John Hope Franklin and Loren Schweninger, *Runway Slaves: Rebels on the Plantation* (New York, 1999); R. J. M. Blackett, *Making Freedom: The Underground Railroad and the Politics of Slavery* (Chapel Hill, NC, 2013).

12. Some of the elements of the process of emancipation have been identified many times over. For example, emancipation generally happened first where slaves and slaveholders were small both in number and in proportion of the population—where slavery was marginal to the economy and peripheral to society. Likewise, where slaves where central to economic production and slaveholders the dominant class, freedom was generally difficult to achieve.

13. Christopher Brown, *Moral Capital: Foundations of British Abolitionism* (Chapel Hill, NC, 2006); James Wavlin, *A Short History of Slavery* (London, 2007), ch. 9; Rebecca Scott, *Slave Emancipation in Cuba: The Transition to Free Labor, 1860–1899* (Princeton, NJ, 1985), 65–66, 111, 123–124; Leslie Bethell, *The Abolition of the Brazilian Slave Trade: Britain, Brazil and the Slave Trade Question, 1807–1869* (Cambridge, UK, 1970); Robert Brent Toplin, *The Abolition of Slavery in Brazil* (New York, 1972).

14. Annette Gordon-Reed, *The Hemingses of Monticello: An American Family* (New York, 2008), ch. 30; Thomas Jefferson, *Notes on the State of Virginia,* ed. William Peden (Chapel Hill, NC, 1954), 163.

15. Many scholars have noted the hardening of sectional lines in the first decade of the nineteenth century, and sometimes even earlier. See, for example,

David Lightner, *Slavery and the Commerce Power: How the Struggle against the Interstate Slave Trade Led to the Civil War* (New Haven, CT, 2006); and Matthew Mason, *Slavery and Politics in the Early Republic* (Chapel Hill, NC, 2006). The same phenomena can be viewed from the Southern perspective. Larry E. Tise, *Proslavery: A History of the Defense of Slavery in America, 1701–1840* (Athens, GA, 1987), ch. 5.

16. The most common periodization of the antislavery movement is the bipartite division between the old abolition movement, which ended slavery in the Northern states by a series of gradualist legislative measures, and a radical movement often said to have begun with the publication of David Walker's *Appeal* in 1829 and William Lloyd Garrison's *Liberator* soon thereafter. Of course, there are finer divisions within the first movement, between the early emancipationists and the colonizationists; and within the second (radical) movement, between Garrisonian antipartisan politics and the politicos of the Liberty, Free Soil, and Republican parties. For a summary of the various ways in which the movement against slavery has been parsed, see Beverly C. Tomek, *Colonization and Its Discontents: Emancipation, Emigration, and Antislavery in Antebellum Pennsylvania* (New York, 2011), 1–4, 13–14; also Richard S. Newman, *The Transformation of American Abolitionism: Fighting Slavery in the Early Republic* (Chapel Hill, NC, 2002), 1–2.

17. Newman, *Transformation of American Abolitionism;* Paul J. Polgar, "'To Raise Them to an Equal Participation':

Early National Abolitionism, Gradual Emancipation, and the Promise of African American Citizenship," *Journal of the Early Republic,* 31 (2011), 229–258; James Brewer Stewart, *Holy Warriors: The Abolitionist and American Slavery,* rev. ed. (New York, 1996), ch. 1; Daniel Walker Howe, "The Evangelical Movement and Political Culture in the North during the Second Party System," *Journal of American History,* 77 (1991), 1216–1239; Merton Dillon, *The Abolitionists: The Growth of a Dissenting Minority* (New York, 1974); Aileen S. Kraditor, *Means and Ends in American Abolitionism: Garrison and His Critics on Strategy and Tactics, 1834–1850* (New York, 1967).

18. Historians of abolition have done what historians do best: trace the changes of the movement over time and place, dividing them into periods, each with its own special characteristics. Steven Hahn, *The Political World of Slavery and Freedom* (Cambridge, MA, 2009), 6, 19. See the historiography parsing "two discrete emancipations."

19. Quoted in Patrick Rael, *Black Identity and Black Protest in the Antebellum North* (Chapel Hill, NC, 2006), 27. Historians have repeatedly made the point—perhaps none more directly than Benjamin Quarles and, recently, Darryl Pinckney—that for white abolitionists the struggle against slavery was ideological warfare, while for black abolitionists it was personal. See Benjamin Quarles, *Black Abolitionists* (New York, 1959), esp. 49–50; Darryl Pinckney, "The Invisibility of Black Abolitionists," in Andrew Delbanco, ed., *The Abolitionist Imagination*

(Cambridge, MA, 2012), 118. The same point was made earlier by W. E. B. Du Bois in *Black Reconstruction in America: An Essay toward a History of the Part which Black Folk Played in the Attempt to Reconstruct Democracy in America* (New York, 1935). Others have taken up the same tradition. See Manisha Sinha, "Coming of Age: The Historiography of Black Abolitionism," in Timothy McCarthy and John Stauffer, eds., *Prophets of Protest: Reconsidering the History of America Abolitionism* (New York, 2006), 23–40; Graham Russell Gao Hodges, *David Ruggles: A Radical Black Abolitionist and the Underground Railroad in New York City* (Chapel Hill, NC, 2010), 79. Ruggles wrote that all black men and women were still "slaves whose condition is but a short remove from that of two million of our race who are pining in their bloody chains" (ibid., 79).

20. Rael, *Black Identity and Black Protest,* 159.

21. Newman, *Transformation of American Abolitionism,* 48–49.

22. Joanne P. Melish identifies the point when "the discourse of slavery had been transformed into the discourse of 'race'": she asserts that the year was 1820. Melish, *Disowning Slavery: Gradual Emancipation and Race in New England, 1780–1860* (Ithaca, NY, 1998), 75–79.

23. Roy P. Basler, ed., *Collected Works of Abraham Lincoln,* 9 vols. (New Brunswick, NJ, 1953), 8:333.

24. *The Liberator,* 3 September 1831.

25. Quoted in Bordewich, *Bound for Canaan,* 225.

26. The point is made most forcefully in Stephen Kantrowitz, *More than Freedom: Fighting for Black Citizenship in a White Republic, 1829–1889* (New York, 2012), 58–99.

27. *Frederick Douglass' Paper,* 15 June 1855; Leon Litwack, "The Emancipation of the Negro Abolitionist," in Martin Duberman, ed., *The Antislavery Vanguard: New Essays on the Abolitionists* (Princeton, NJ, 1965), 148–149; also Quarles, *Black Abolitionists,* 169.

28. Michael P. Johnson, "Denmark Vesey and His Co-Conspirators," *William and Mary Quarterly,* 58 (2001), 915–976; Douglas R. Egerton, "Forgetting Denmark Vesey; or, Oliver Stone Meets Richard Wade," *William and Mary Quarterly,* 59 (2002), 143–152.

29. Carter G. Woodson, *Free Negro Owners of Slaves in the United States in 1830* (1924; rpt. Westport, CT, 1973); R. Halliburton, Jr., "Free Black Owners of Slaves: A Reappraisal of the Woodson Thesis," *South Carolina Historical Magazine,* 76 (1976), 129–142; David L. Lightner and Alexander M. Ragan, "Were African American Slaveholders Benevolent or Exploitative? A Quantitative Approach," *Journal of Southern History,* 71 (2005), 535–558; Larry Koger, *Black Slaveowners: Free Black Slave Masters in South Carolina, 1790–1860* (Jefferson, NC, 1985).

30. Laurent Dubois, *Avengers of the New World: The Story of the Haitian Revolution* (Cambridge, MA, 2004), 176–180.

31. David Brion Davis, *The Problem of Slavery in Western Culture* (Ithaca, NY, 1966), pt. 3.

32. Berlin, *Slaves without Masters,* ch. 8; Julie Winch, *A Gentleman of Color: The Life of James Forten* (New York, 2002), 89, 129–130.

33. William Cain, ed., *William Lloyd Garrison and the Fight against Slavery* (Boston, 1995), 14. See, more generally, Quarles, *Black Abolitionists;* and Rael, *Black Identity and Black Protest.*

34. Richard Newman, "Protest in Black and White: The Formation and Transformation of an African American Political Community during the Early Republic," in Jeffrey Pasley et al., *Beyond the Founders: New Approaches to the Political History of the Early American Republic* (Chapel Hill, NC, 2004), 185; also Leon F. Litwack, *North of Slavery: The Negroes in the Free States, 1790–1860* (Chicago, 1961), 223–226.

35. David Brion Davis has written that free blacks "provided the key to slave emancipation." See Davis, *The Problem of Slavery in the Age of Emancipation* (New York, 2014), xiv. Also Quarles, *Black Abolitionists,* 81–86.

36. Judith N. Shklar, *American Citizenship: The Quest for Inclusion* (Cambridge, MA, 1991); Linda Kerber, *No Constitutional Right to Be Ladies: Women and the Obligations of Citizenship* (New York, 1998), 47–80.

37. Rael, *Black Identity and Black Protest,* ch. 5.

38. John Thornton, "Africa and Abolitionism," in Seymour Drescher and Pieter C. Emmer, eds., *Who Abolished Slavery? Slave Revolts and Abolitionism: A Debate with João Pedro Marques* (New York, 2010), 95–96.

39. Quoted in Rael, *Black Identity and Black Protest*, 12 and ch. 1.

40. Dixon Ryan Fox, "The Negro Vote in Old New York," *Political Science Quarterly*, 32 (1917), 252–275; David Gellman and David Quigley, eds., *Jim Crow New York: A Documentary History of Race and Citizenship, 1777–1877* (New York, 2003), 58–63.

41. Barbara J. Fields, "Ideology and Race in American History," in J. Morgan Kouser and James M. McPherson, eds., *Region, Race, and Reconstruction: Essays in Honor of C. Vann Woodward* (New York, 1982), 143–178.

42. James Forten, *A Series of Letters by a Man of Color* (Philadelphia, 1813), 1, 3.

2. Sounding the Egalitarian Clarion

1. Pauline Maier, *American Scripture: Making the Declaration of Independence* (New York, 1997); David Armitage, *The Declaration of Independence: A Global History* (Cambridge, MA, 2007); Alexander Tsesis, *For Liberty and Equality: The Life and Times of the Declaration of Independence* (New York, 2012), chs. 3–4.

2. Christine Heyrman, *Southern Cross: The Beginnings of the Bible Belt* (New York, 1997), ch. 1. The Society of Friends triumphed over the secular opponents of slavery. Believing that all people shared a spark of God's divinity and hence were equally free, they began to eradicate slavery within their religious community in the 1750s.

3. For two very different explorations of how notions

of equality shaped society in the early American republic, see Alfred F. Young, *The American Revolution: Explorations in the History of American Radicalism* (Dekalb, IL, 1976); Gordon S. Wood, *The Radicalism of the American Revolution* (New York, 1992).

4. Francis Newton Thorpe, comp., *The Federal and State Constitutions,* 7 vols. (Washington, DC, 1909), 3:1888 (Massachusetts); 4:2453 (New Hampshire); 5:2653 (New York); 7:3812 (Virginia).

5. Bernard Bailyn, *The Ideological Origins of the American Revolution,* rev. ed. (Cambridge, MA, 1992), makes the case for the "contagion of liberty." Quote from "Brief of Levi Lincoln in the Slave Case Tried in 1781," *Collections of the Massachusetts Historical Society,* 5th ser., vol. 3 (1877), 440.

6. Orlando Patterson, *Slavery and Social Death: A Comparative History* (Cambridge, MA, 1982).

7. Benjamin Quarles, *The Negro in the American Revolution* (Chapel Hill, NC, 1961), 38–40, 98, 142–152; Sylvia R. Frey, *Water from the Rock: Black Resistance in a Revolutionary Age* (Princeton, NJ, 1991), 108, 28–29; Sylvia R. Frey, "Between Slavery and Freedom: Virginia Blacks in the American Revolution," *Journal of Southern History,* 49 (1983), 389–404; Shane White, *Somewhat More Independent: The End of Slavery in New York City, 1770–1810* (Athens, GA, 1991), 130–131.

8. Gary B. Nash, *The Forgotten Fifth: African Americans in the Age of Revolution* (Cambridge, MA, 2006), 10; Gary B. Nash and Jean R. Soderlund, *Freedom by Degrees:*

Emancipation in Philadelphia and Its Aftermath (New York, 1991), 94, 96. For Lincoln's words, see Roy P. Basler, ed., *The Collected Works of Abraham Lincoln,* 9 vols. (New Brunswick, NJ, 1953–1955), 7:271–272.

9. Nash, *The Forgotten Fifth,* 17–19; Frey, *Water from the Rock,* 108, 28–29: Quarles, *The Negro in the American Revolution,* 77, 89, 134, 140–142, 152.

10. Roger Bruns, *Am I Not a Man and a Brother: The Antislavery Crusade of Revolutionary America, 1688–1788* (New York, 1977), 428, 452–456; Thomas J. Davis, "Emancipation Rhetoric: Natural Rights and Revolutionary New England: A Note on Four Black Petitions in Massachusetts, 1773–1777," *New England Quarterly,* 62 (1989), 248–263; "Petitions of Several Poor Negroes and Mulattoes," in George Washington Williams, *History of the Negro Race in America, 1619–1880* (New York, 1968), 184; Herbert Aptheker, ed., *A Documentary History of the Negro People in the United States,* 2 vols. (New York, 1994), 1:5–12; Edgar J. McManus, *Black Bondage in the North* (Syracuse, NY, 1973), 171.

11. Michael L. Nicholls, "'The Squint of Freedom': African-American Freedom Suits in Post-Revolutionary Virginia," *Slavery and Abolition,* 20 (1999), 47–62; T. Stephen Whitman, *Challenging Slavery in the Chesapeake: Black and White Resistance to Human Bondage, 1775–1865* (Baltimore, 2007), 80–84; Loren Schweninger, "Freedom Suits, African American Women, and the Genealogy of Slavery," *William and Mary Quarterly,* 71 (2014), 41–42; Peter Wallenstein, "Indian Foremothers: Race, Sex, Slavery,

and Freedom in Early Virginia," in Catherine Clinton and Michele Gillespie, eds., *The Devil's Lane: Sex and Race in the Early South* (New York, 1997), 57–73; Honor Sachs, "'Freedom by a Judgment': The Legacy and History of an Afro-Indian Family," *Law and History Review,* 30 (2012), 173–203.

12. The legal record of Irish Nell's suit can be followed in http://msa.maryland.gov/megafile/msa/speccol/sc5400 /sc5496/000500/000534/html/00534bio.html.

13. Schweninger, "Freedom Suits, African American Women, and the Genealogy of Slavery," 42. On the importance of "common knowledge," "hearsay evidence," and the slaves' own recollections of their genealogy, see Sachs, "Freedom by a Judgment," 173–202; Jason A. Gillmer, "Suing for Freedom: Interracial Sex, Slave Law, and Racial Identity in the Post-Revolutionary and Antebellum South," *North Carolina Law Review,* 82 (2004), 535–620. Also see Lea Vandervelde, *Redemption Songs: Suing for Freedom before Dred Scott* (New York, 2014).

14. William M. Wiecek, "*Somerset:* Lord Mansfield and the Legitimacy of Slavery in the Anglo-American World," *University of Chicago Law Review,* 42 (1974), 86–146; George W. Van Cleve, *A Slaveholders' Union: Slavery, Politics, and the Constitution in the Early American Republic* (Chicago, 2010), 31–40; Steven M. Wise, *Though the Heavens May Fall: The Landmark Trial that Led to the End of Human Slavery* (Cambridge, MA, 2005).

15. William O'Brien, "Did the Jenison Case Outlaw Slavery in Massachusetts?" *William and Mary Quarterly,*

17 (1960), 219–241; John D. Cushing, "The Cushing Court and the Abolition of Slavery in Massachusetts: More Notes on the 'Quok Walker Case,' " *American Journal of Legal History,* 5 (1961), 118–144; Arthur Zilversmit, "Quok Walker, Mumbet, and the Abolition of Slavery in Massachusetts," *William and Mary Quarterly,* 25 (1968), 614–624; Elaine MacEacheren, "Emancipation of Slavery in Massachusetts: A Reexamination, 1770–1790," *Journal of Negro History,* 55 (1970), 289–306; Joanne P. Melish, *Disowning Slavery: Gradual Emancipation and Race in New England, 1780–1860* (Ithaca, NY, 1998), 64–66.

16. Arthur Zilversmit, *The First Emancipation: The Abolition of Slavery in the North* (Chicago, 1967), 101–105, 114–123.

17. Davis, "Emancipation Rhetoric: Natural Rights and Revolutionary New England," 248–263; Bruns, *Am I Not a Man and a Brother,* 428, 452–456.

18. Aptheker, ed., *A Documentary History of the Negro People,* 1:5–12; Bruns, *Am I Not a Man and a Brother,* 474–475; McManus, *Black Bondage in the North,* 171; Richard S. Newman, *The Transformation of American Abolitionism: Fighting Slavery in the Early Republic* (Chapel Hill, NC, 2002), 89.

19. Thorpe, comp., *The Federal and State Constitutions,* 4:2453 (New Hampshire); 6:3739 (Vermont); Melish, *Disowning Slavery,* 93–95, 107–108, 110–111. On the final demise of slavery in New Hampshire, see note 31 below.

20. Thorpe, comp., *The Federal and State Constitutions,* 3:1889 (Massachusetts); 4:2453 (New Hampshire); 7:3813 (Virginia).

21. H. Robert Baker, "The Fugitive Slave Clause and the Antebellum Constitution," *Law and History Review,* 30 (2012), 1133–38; Don E. Fehrenbacher, *The Slaveholding Republic: An Account of the United States Government's Relations to Slavery* (New York, 2002), 211–215, 240–241; Van Cleve, *Slaveholders' Union,* part 3, esp. 189–191.

22. Van Cleve, *Slaveholders' Union,* 71–79; David N. Gellman, *Emancipating New York: The Politics of Slavery and Freedom, 1777–1827* (Baton Rouge, LA, 2006), 49; Robert William Fogel and Stanley E. Engerman, "Philanthropy at Bargain Prices: Notes on the Economics of Gradual Emancipation," *Journal of Legal Studies,* 3 (1974), 377–401; Melish, *Disowning Slavery,* 90–95.

23. Melish, *Disowning Slavery,* 69–71, 76. Melish notes that the post-nati laws invented "an entirely new form of servitude." Unlike indentureship, post-nati servitude was noncontractual. It placed binding requirements only on the worker, and none on the "owner." Those assigned a post-nati status lived in an "undefined limbo of mandatory, uncompensated service: not a slave, not contractually bound, not free."

24. Zilversmit, *The First Emancipation,* 126, 143; Van Cleve, *Slaveholders' Union,* 66–68.

25. David Gellman has asserted that "speech could make the man, or even the race"; see his insightful discussion of the use of racial invective in denying

black people a place in the public sphere (Gellman, *Emancipating New York,* ch. 6, quotation on 104); also Zilversmit, *The First Emancipation,* 134–135: Paul J. Polgar, " 'To Raise Them to an Equal Participation': Early National Abolitionism, Gradual Emancipation, and the Promise of African American Citizenship," *Journal of the Early Republic,* 31 (2011), 237.

26. *New York Packet* quoted in Gellman, *Emancipating New York,* 53–54; Polgar, "To Raise Them to an Equal Participation," 253.

27. Paul J. Polgar, "To Raise Them to an Equal Participation," 229–258; and Paul J. Polgar, "Standard Bearers of Liberty and Equality: Reinterpreting the Origins of American Abolitionism" (doctoral diss., City University of New York, 2013), chs. 2–4.

28. Nash and Soderlund, *Freedom by Degrees,* ch. 2, quotations on 100–101.

29. Van Cleve, *Slaveholders' Union,* 63–66; Nash and Soderlund, *Freedom by Degrees,* ch. 4. On the final demise of slavery in Pennsylvania, see note 31 below.

30. *First Annual Report of the New York Committee of Vigilance for the Year 1837* (New York, 1837), 14; Melish, *Disowning Slavery,* ch. 2. Lewis Gerrard Clarke was just one of many fugitives to conclude that "the *spirit* of slaveholding was not all South of the Ohio River." Quoted in Steven Hahn, *The Political Worlds of Slavery and Freedom* (Cambridge, MA, 2009), 1; also see 1–5.

31. Melish, *Disowning Slavery,* 70. Putting the final nail in slavery's coffin, however, took time. In New York,

slavery was not legally dead until 1827; in New Jersey, until 1846; in Pennsylvania, until 1847; in Connecticut, until 1848; and in New Hampshire, until 1857.

32. David Brion Davis, *The Problem of Slavery in Western Culture* (Ithaca, NY, 1966), part 3; Zilversmit, *The First Emancipation.*

33. White, *Somewhat More Independent,* 150–153; Shane White, *Stories of Freedom in Black New York* (Cambridge, MA, 2002), 45–46; Gellman, *Emancipating New York,* 195.

34. Zilversmit, *The First Emancipation,* 226–227; Van Cleve, *Slaveholders' Union,* 61, estimates that 70 percent of Northern slaves lived in jurisdictions where gradual abolition was contested.

35. Van Cleve, *Slaveholders' Union,* 79–92; Melish, *Disowning Slavery,* ch. 3, esp. 94–98; Zilversmit, *The First Emancipation,* 136; Nash and Soderlund, *Freedom by Degrees,* 112; Gellman, *Emancipating New York,* 205.

36. Newman, *Transformation of American Abolitionism,* 24; Nash and Soderlund, *Freedom by Degrees,* 3–4, 104, 135; Gellman, *Emancipating New York,* 195.

37. Fogel and Engerman, "Philanthropy at Bargain Prices," 377–401.

38. Melish, *Disowning Slavery,* 90–92, cites numerous examples of freedom suits in which slave children did not know their age. Gellman, *Emancipating New York,* 66–67; James J. Gigantino, "Trading in Jersey Souls: New Jersey and the Interstate Slave Trade," *Pennsylvania History,* 77 (2010), 282. In 1788, and again in 1812, New Jersey lawmakers mandated that slaves had to give their

consent in order to be sold and transferred out of state. While those laws may have allowed the prospective free men and women (slaves for a term, according to New Jersey law) the "right to determine at least some of the direction of their own lives," the laws were frequently ignored or consent was obtained by force (ibid., 283).

39. Nash and Soderlund, *Freedom by Degrees,* 138; Melish, *Disowning Slavery,* 89–118. According to economist Claudia Golden, as many as two-thirds of New York's slaves never gained their promised freedom. Claudia D. Golden, "The Economics of Emancipation," *Journal of Economic History,* 33 (1973), 70.

40. Nash and Soderlund, *Freedom by Degrees,* 114–116; *Minutes of the Proceedings of the Seventh Convention of Delegates from the Abolition Societies* (Philadelphia, 1801), 14, 40.

41. Carol Wilson, *Freedom at Risk: The Kidnapping of Free Blacks in America, 1780–1865* (Lexington, KY, 1994); Daniel Meaders, *Kidnappers in Philadelphia: Isaac Hopper's Tales of Oppression, 1780–1843* (Cherry Hill, NJ, 2009); Nash and Soderlund, *Freedom by Degrees,* 196–200 and note 37.

42. *Poulson's American Daily Advertiser* (Philadelphia), 3 July 1818; *Westchester Village Record* (Pennsylvania), 15 July 1819; both cited in Nash and Soderlund, *Freedom by Degrees,* 200.

43. Ibid.

44. Ibid.

45. Graham Russell Gao Hodges, *Slavery and Freedom in the Rural North: African Americans in Monmouth County, New Jersey, 1665–1865* (Madison, WI, 1997), 118–121; Nash and Soderlund, *Freedom by Degrees*, 199–200.

46. Paul Finkelman, "The Kidnapping of John Davis and the Adoption of the Fugitive Slave Law of 1793," *Journal of Southern History,* 56 (1990), 419–420; Paul Finkelman, *An Imperfect Union: Slavery, Federalism, and Comity* (Chapel Hill, NC, 1981); Van Cleve, *Slaveholders' Union,* 24–25; Melish, *Disowning Slavery,* 99–101.

47. White, *Somewhat More Independent,* 108–112, 115, 149–152; White, *Stories of Freedom in Black New York,* 8–66; Vivienne L. Kruger, "Born to Run: The Slave Family in Early New York, 1626–1827" (doctoral diss., Columbia University, 1985), 725, 742, 748, 755–766; Gellman, *Emancipating New York,* 194–197.

48. Newman, *Transformation of American Abolitionism,* chs. 2–3; Polgar, "To Raise Them to an Equal Participation," 229–258; Van Cleve, *Slaveholders' Union,* 82; Nash and Soderlund, *Freedom by Degrees,* 80, 99, 127–128, 132–134; Gellman, *Emancipating New York,* ch. 4, esp.161–165.

49. Newman, *Transformation of American Abolitionism,* ch. 2; Polgar, "To Raise Them to an Equal Participation," 229–258; Henry Cabot Lodge, ed., *The Works of Alexander Hamilton,* 12 vols. (New York, 1904), 9:160–161; Bruns, *Am I Not a Man and a Brother,* 443–445; Gellman, *Emancipating New York,* 9, ch. 2; Peter Hinks, "Timothy

Dwight, Congregationalism, and Early Antislavery," in Steven Mintz and John Stauffer, eds., *The Problem of Evil: Slavery, Freedom, and the Ambiguities of American Reform* (Amherst, MA, 2007), 155–158.

50. Polgar, "To Raise Them to an Equal Participation," 229–258, quotations on 250.

51. Nash and Soderlund, *Freedom by Degrees,* 132–134.

52. Patrick Rael, *Black Identity and Black Protest in the Antebellum North* (Chapel Hill, NC, 2002), 60–78; White, *Somewhat More Independent,* ch. 5; Billy G. Smith and Richard Wojtowicz, eds., *Blacks Who Stole Themselves: Advertisements for Runaways in the Pennsylvania Gazette, 1728–1790* (Philadelphia, 1989); Nash and Soderlund, *Freedom by Degrees,* 37, 76–77, 95, 141.

53. White, *Somewhat More Independent,* 117–119.

54. Ibid., 132, 145–147, 155; Gellman, *Emancipating New York,* 145–146.

55. Laurent Dubois, *Avenger of the New World: The Story of the Haitian Revolution* (Cambridge, MA, 2004), 176–177; Ashli White, *Encounter Revolution: Haiti and the Making of the Early Republic* (Baltimore, 2010), 125–126, 134–136, 145–146.

56. Martha S. Jones, "Time, Space, and Jurisdiction in Atlantic World Slavery: The Volunbrun Household in Gradual Emancipation New York," *Law and History Review,* 20 (2011), 1031–60; and Martha S. Jones, "The Case of Jean Baptiste, un Créole de Saint-Domingue: Narrating Slavery, Freedom, and the Haitian Revolution in Baltimore City," in Brian Ward, Martin Bone, and

William A. Link, eds., *The American South and the Atlantic World* (Gainesville, FL, 2013), 104–128.

57. *First Annual Report of the New York Committee of Vigilance for the Year 1837* (New York, 1837), 14.

58. Leon F. Litwack, *North of Slavery: The Negroes in the Free States, 1790–1860* (Chicago, 1961), 18; James O. Horton and Lois E. Horton, *In Hopes of Liberty: Culture, Community, and Protest among Northern Free Blacks, 1700–1860* (New York, 1997), 100, 174, 180; Stephen Kantrowitz, *More than Freedom: Fighting for Black Citizenship in a White Republic, 1829–1889* (New York, 2012); Craig Wilder, *In the Company of Black Men: The African Influence on African American Culture in New York City* (New York, 2001).

59. Kantrowitz, *More than Freedom*, 7, 24.

60. Peter S. Onuf, " 'To Declare Them a Free and Independent People': Race, Slavery, and National Identity in Jefferson's Thought," *Journal of the Early Republic,* 18 (1998), note 1.

61. Thomas Jefferson, *Notes on the State of Virginia,* ed. William Peden (Chapel Hill, NC, 1954), 163, 143.

62. Thomas Jefferson, "Autobiography Draft Fragment," 27 July 1821, in Paul Leicester Ford, ed., *The Works of Thomas Jefferson,* 12 vols. (New York, 1904–1905), 12 (27 July 1821); Jefferson, *Notes on the State of Virginia,* 138, 163.

63. Peter Onuf notes that Jefferson's generalizations about racial characteristics, most provocatively in his *Notes on the State of Virginia,* may have "set the pattern

for modern American racism." Certainly this pattern is most evident in the 1790s. Onuf, "To Declare Them a Free and Independent People," 17.

64. Jefferson was not alone in his view of that people of African descent were physically and mentally different from and inferior to whites. For a long list of Enlightenment thinkers who endorsed this view, see Emmanuel Chukwudi Eze, ed., *Race and the Enlightenment: A Reader* (Cambridge, MA, 1997).

65. Paul Finkelman, *Slavery and the Founders: Race and Liberty in the Age of Jefferson,* 2nd ed. (Armonk, NY, 2001), ch. 1; Robin L. Einhorn, *American Taxation, American Slavery* (Chicago, 2006); Van Cleve, *Slaveholders' Union,* 8–9, 103–186.

66. Litwack, *North of Slavery,* 30–32, 58; Kantrowitz, *More than Freedom,* 36.

67. *Annals of Congress,* 1 Cong., 2 Sess., 19 February 1798, 1239–40; Newman, *Transformation of American Abolitionism,* ch. 2; Richard S. Newman, "Prelude to the Gag Rule: Southern Reaction to Antislavery Petitions on the First Federal Congress," *Journal of the Early Republic,* 16 (1996), 571–600.

68. Howard A. Ohline, "Slavery, Economics, and Congressional Politics, 1790," *Journal of Southern History,* 46 (1980), 335–360, quotation on 355; Van Cleve, *Slaveholders' Union,* 191–203.

69. *Annals of Congress,* 1 Cong., 2 Sess., 1505; Ohline, "Slavery, Economics, and Congressional Politics," 342–345, 348–353; Newman, *Transformation of American*

Abolitionism, 55–59; Van Cleve, *Slaveholders' Union,* 98. For an antislavery New Yorker's commentary on the congressional debate, as well Franklin's last words, see Gellman, *Emancipating New York,* 96–101.

70. Quoted in Eva Sheppard Wolf, *Race and Liberty in the New Nation: Emancipation in Virginia, from the Revolution to Nat Turner's Rebellion* (Baton Rouge, LA, 2006), 1.

71. While there seems no doubt about the explosive growth of Virginia's free black population in the years following the Revolution, the size and source of that increase have been disputed. Eva Sheppard Wolf discounts St. George Tucker's estimate of a free black population of 1,800 prior to the Revolution, and maintains that no more than 10,000 slaves were manumitted in Virginia between the Revolution and 1810, when the census total was about 30,000. She believes that the prewar free black population was much more substantial, perhaps as many as 5,500, and that much of the growth of the free black population in the post-Revolutionary period stemmed from this group (Wolf, *Race and Liberty in the New Nation,* 44–45). Others have stood by Tucker's estimate and his view that manumission was a primary source of the expanding free black population (Berlin, *Slaves without Masters,* 29–35, 46–47). The best study of manumission in post-Revolutionary Virginia is Peter J. Albert, "The Protean Institution: Geography, Economy, and Ideology of Slavery in Post-Revolutionary Virginia (doctoral diss., University of Maryland, 1976).

72. Sachs, "Freedom by a Judgment," 176–177, 192–202.

73. Newman, *Transformation of American Abolitionism*, 37–38; Winthrop D. Jordan, *White over Black: American Attitudes toward the Negro, 1550–1812* (Chapel Hill, NC, 1968), 555–561; Van Cleve, *Slaveholders' Union*, 206–208, quotation on 207; Wolf, *Race and Liberty*, 101, 104–107; St. George Tucker, *A Dissertation on Slavery with a Proposal for the Gradual Abolition of It, in the State of Virginia* (Philadelphia, 1796).

74. Douglas R. Egerton, *Gabriel's Rebellion: The Virginia Slave Conspiracies of 1800 and 1802* (Chapel Hill, NC, 1993), 163; Michael L. Nicholls, *Whispers of Rebellion: Narrating Gabriel's Conspiracy* (Charlottesville, VA, 2012); James Sidbury, *Ploughshares into Swords: Race, Rebellion and Identity in Gabriel's Virginia, 1730–1810* (Cambridge, UK, 1997), 134–135, 138; Philip J. Schwarz, ed., *Gabriel's Conspiracy: A Documentary History* (Charlottesville, VA, 2012).

75. Wolf, *Race and Liberty*, ch. 2; quotation in *Virginia Argus* (Richmond), 17 January 1806.

76. Ira Berlin, *Generations of Captivity: A History of African-American Slaves* (Cambridge, MA, 2003), 272–279.

77. On the rise of black political awareness, see Rael, *Black Identity and Black Protest;* James Brewer Stewart, "The Emergence of Racial Modernity and the Rise of the White North, 1790–1840," *Journal of the Early Republic,* 18 (1998), 181–217; John Sweet Wood, *Bodies Politic:*

Negotiating Race in the American North, 1730–1830 (Baltimore, 2003), 243–267.

78. Schwarz, ed., *Gabriel's Conspiracy: A Documentary History*, xiv, 35, 54, 274–281.

79. Daniel Rasmussen, *American Uprising: The Untold Story of America's Largest Slave Revolt* (New York, 2011).

80. On the distinction between the first generation of white abolitionists and the white colonizationists, see Polgar, "To Raise Them to an Equal Participation," 257–258.

3. The Bloody Struggle Endures

1. Thomas Slaughter, *Bloody Dawn: The Christiana Riot and Racial Violence in the Antebellum North* (New York, 1991), 49; Ira Berlin, *Generations of Captivity: A History of African-American Slaves* (Cambridge, MA, 2003), 233–237; Steven Hahn, *The Political World of Slavery and Freedom* (Cambridge, MA, 2009), 22–44.

2. Don E. Fehrenbacher, *The Slaveholding Republic: An Account of the United States Government's Relations to Slavery*, completed and edited by Ward M. McAfree (New York, 2001); David F. Ericson, *Slavery and the American Republic: Developing the Federal Government, 1791–1861* (Lawrence, KS, 2011); Lacy K. Ford, *Deliver Us from Evil: The Slavery Question in the Old South* (New York, 2009), part 4.

3. Joanne P. Melish, *Disowning Slavery: Gradual Emancipation and Race in New England, 1780–1860*

(Ithaca, NY, 1998), 215–216; Robert P. Forbes, *The Missouri Compromise and Its Aftermath: Slavery and the Meaning of America* (Chapel Hill, NC, 2007), 107.

4. When it came to tweaking white Northerners and refuting their claim that black people would take advantage of the opportunities of freedom, perhaps no Southern politician was more effective than James Henry Hammond. Drew Gilpin Faust, *James Henry Hammond and the Old South: A Design for Mastery* (New Orleans, 1982), 176–177.

5. Matthew Mason, *Slavery and Politics in the Early American Republic* (Chapel Hill, NC, 2006), 145–150.

6. The best account of the Missouri Debates is Forbes, *The Missouri Compromise*, chs. 2–3, quotation on 38.

7. Ibid., quotations on 39, 40.

8. Ibid., ch. 2, quotation on 44. On Northern representatives' preoccupation with economic rather than moral questions, see George Van Cleve, *A Slaveholders' Union: Slavery, Politics, and the Constitution of the Early American Republic* (Chicago, 2010), ch. 4.

9. On the growth of free black society, see Richard Newman, "Protest in Black and White: The Formation and Transformation of an African American Political Community during the Early Republic," in Jeffrey Pasley et al., eds., *Beyond the Founders: New Approaches to the Political History of the Early American Republic* (Chapel Hill, NC, 2004), 184–187; James Oliver Horton and Lois E. Horton, *In Hope of Liberty: Culture, Community, and Protest among Northern Free Blacks, 1700–1860* (New York, 1997);

John Ernest, *A Nation within a Nation: Organizing African American Communities before the Civil War* (Chicago, 2011); Stephen Kantrowitz, *More than Freedom: Fighting for Black Citizenship in a White Republic, 1829–1889* (New York, 2012), introduction; Carla Peterson, "Black Life in Freedom: Creating an Elite Culture," in Ira Berlin and Leslie Harris, eds., *Slavery in New York* (New York, 2005), 184–204; Joanna Brooks, "The Early American Public Sphere and the Emergence of a Black Print Counterpublic," *William and Mary Quarterly,* 62 (2005), 67–92.

10. *Freedom's Journal* (New York), 16 March 1827; Winston James, *The Struggles of John Brown Russwurm: The Life and Writings of a Pan-Africanist Pioneer, 1799–1851* (New York, 2010).

11. This point is made most clearly by Newman, "Protest in Black and White," 192.

12. Douglas R. Egerton, " 'Its Origin Is Not a Little Curious': A New Look at the American Colonization Society," *Journal of the Early Republic,* 5 (1985), 463–480.

13. Quoted in Leon F. Litwack, *North of Slavery: The Negroes in the Free States, 1790–1860* (Chicago, 1961), 21; *The African Repository and Colonial Journal,* 1 (1825), 68.

14. Julie Winch, *A Gentleman of Color: The Life of James Forten* (New York, 2002), ch. 8 and 190–192, 235–237.

15. Lionel Kennedy and Thomas Parker, eds., *An Official Report of the Trial of Sundry Negroes, Charged with an Attempt to Raise an Insurrection in the State of South Carolina* (Charleston, SC, 1822), 19; Michael P. Johnson,

"Denmark Vesey and His Co-Conspirators," *William and Mary Quarterly,* 58 (2001), 915–976; also the Forum on Vesey in volume 59 of the *William and Mary Quarterly;* John Lofton, *Insurrection in South Carolina: The Turbulent World of Denmark Vesey* (Yellow Springs, OH, 1964); Douglas R. Egerton, *He Shall Go Out Free: The Lives of Denmark Vesey,* rev. ed. (Lanham, MD, 2004).

16. David Walker, "David Walker Addresses the Massachusetts General Colored Association, 1828," in Peter P. Hinks, ed., *David Walker's Appeal to the Coloured Citizens of the World* (University Park, PA, 2006), 85–89.

17. Ibid., 112.

18. Ibid., 28 and esp. the introduction; Peter P. Hinks, *To Awaken My Afflicted Brethren: David Walker and the Problem of Antebellum Slave Resistance* (University Park, PA, 1997).

19. Hinks, ed., *David Walker's Appeal,* 17.

20. Quoted ibid., 32.

21. John L. Thomas, *The Liberator: William Lloyd Garrison* (Boston, 1963), 94; Hinks, ed., *David Walker's Appeal,* xli–xliv; Richard S. Newman, *The Transformation of American Abolitionism: Fighting Slavery in the Early American Republic* (Chapel Hill, NC, 2002), 114–115.

22. *The Liberator* (Boston), 1 January 1831; Newman, *Transformation of American Abolitionism,* 115–120; William Lloyd Garrison, *Thoughts on African Colonization* (Boston, 1832).

23. Quoted in *The Liberator,* 4 July 1835.

24. Thomas, *The Liberator,* 457–458; Donald M. Jacobs, "David Walker and William Lloyd Garrison: Racial Cooperation and the Shaping of Boston Abolition," in Jacobs, ed., *Courage and Conscience: Black and White Abolitionists in Boston* (Bloomington, IN, 1993), 1–20; quotation in *The Liberator,* 4 July 1835.

25. Michael Feldberg, *The Turbulent Era: Riot and Disorder in Jacksonian America* (New York, 1980); Leonard P. Richards, *"Gentlemen of Property and Standing": Anti-Abolition Mobs in Jacksonian America* (New York, 1970); David Grimsted, *American Mobbing, 1828–1861* (New York, 1998), chs. 2–5.

26. Thomas D. Morris, *Free Men All: Personal Liberty Laws of the North, 1780–1861* (Baltimore, 1974); William M. Wiecek, *The Sources of Antislavery Constitutionalism in American, 1780–1848* (Ithaca, NY, 1977), 159–162.

27. Graham Russell Gao Hodges, *David Ruggles: A Radical Black Abolitionist and the Underground Railroad in New York City* (Chapel Hill, NC, 2010), 93; Peter P. Hinks, " 'Frequently Plunged into Slavery': Free Blacks and Kidnapping in Antebellum Boston," *Historical Journal of Massachusetts,* 20 (1992), 16–31.

28. James J. Gigantino, "Trading in Jersey Souls: New Jersey and the Interstate Slave Trade," *Pennsylvania History,* 77 (2010), 281–295, quotation on 291.

29. Hodges, *David Ruggles,* 50–62, 87–100.

30. Linda K. Kerber, "Abolitionists and Amalgamators: The New York City Race Riots of 1834," *New York*

History, 48 (1967), 28–39; Emma Jones Lapsansky, "'Since They Got Those Separate Churches': Afro-American and Racism in Jacksonian Philadelphia," *American Quarterly,* 32 (1980), 54–78; John Runcie, "'Hunting the Nigs' in Philadelphia: The Race Riot of August 1834," *Pennsylvania History,* 39 (1972), 187–218; Nikki Taylor, "Reconsidering the 'Forced' Exodus of 1829: Free Black Emigration from Cincinnati, Ohio, to Wilberforce, Canada," *Journal of African American History,* 87 (2002), 283–302; John M. Werner, *Reaping the Bloody Harvest: Race Riots in the United States during the Age of Jackson, 1824–1849* (New York, 1986); Leonard L. Richards, *Gentleman of Property and Standing: Anti-Abolition Mobs in Jacksonian America* (New York, 1970), 14–15.

31. *First Annual Report of the New York Committee of Vigilance for the Year 1837* (New York, 1837), 7, 3; William Still, *The Underground Railroad,* rev. ed. (Philadelphia, 1878), 674–675; Hodges, *David Ruggles,* 88, 94; Paul J. Polgar, "Remaking American Antislavery: The Ideological Departure of the American Colonization Society and the Response of Early Abolitionists," paper delivered at the Washington Area Early American Seminar, University of Maryland (22 November 2013), 14–15.

32. Hinks, ed., *David Walker's Appeal,* 28.

33. Hodges, *David Ruggles,* 36; Shane White, *Stories of Freedom in Black New York* (Cambridge, MA, 2002), 25–30; R. J. M. Blackett, *Making Freedom: The Underground Railroad and the Politics of Slavery* (Chapel Hill, NC, 2013), 34–35.

34. Quoted in Hodges, *David Ruggles,* 43.

35. Eric Foner, *Gateway to Freedom: The Hidden History of the Underground Railroad* (New York, 2015), 65, 79, 89, quotation on 77; Larry Gara, *The Liberty Line: The Legend of the Underground Railroad* (Lexington, KY, 1967).

36. Blackett, *Making Freedom,* ch. 2; Mary D. Houts, "Black Harrisburg's Resistance to Slavery," *Pennsylvania Heritage,* 4 (1977); Gerald G. Eggert, "The Impact of the Fugitive Slave Law on Harrisburg: A Case Study," *Pennsylvania Magazine of History and Biography,* 109 (1985), 537–569; Joseph A. Borome, "The Vigilance Committee of Philadelphia," *Pennsylvania Magazine of History and Biography,* 92 (1968), 320–352.

37. Newman, "Protest in Black and White," 185, 197; C. Peter Riply et al., eds., *Black Abolitionist Papers,* 5 vols., (Chapel Hill, NC, 1985–1991), 3:216–220 (nos. 19–20).

38. Quoted in *The Works of James McCune Smith, Black Intellectual and Abolitionist,* ed. John Stauffer (New York, 2006), 154; Douglass quoted in Foner, *Gateway to Freedom,* 145.

39. Hodges, *David Ruggles,* 90, 94; Blackett, *Making Freedom,* ch. 1, esp. 5–6; Steven Hahn, *A Nation under Our Feet: Black Political Struggles in the Rural South from Slavery to the Great Migration* (Cambridge, MA, 2002), 55–57.

40. John Hope Franklin and Loren Schweninger, *Runway Slaves: Rebels on the Plantation* (New York, 1999), ch. 6, pp. 88, 145.

41. Ibid., 11, 78, 84, 211, 262; Blackett, *Making Freedom,* 32.

42. Max Grivno, *Gleanings of Freedom: Free and Slave Labor along the Mason-Dixon Line, 1790–1860* (Urbana, IL, 2011), 24–27, 70–72, 155–156.

43. Ibid., 75–77, 127–131, quotations on 77.

44. Ibid., 129–131, quotations on 129.

45. M. Scott Heerman, "Deep River: Slavery, Empire, and Emancipation in the Upper Mississippi River Valley, 1730–1860" (doctoral diss., University of Maryland, 2013), 244–248.

46. Stanley Harrold, *Border War: Fighting over Slavery before the Civil War* (Chapel Hill, NC, 2010), quotation on 14.

47. Fehrenbacher, *Slaveholding Republic,* 231; H. Robert Baker, "The Fugitive Slave Clause and Antebellum Constitutionalism," *Law and History Review,* 30 (2012), 1133–74; Steven Lubet, *Fugitive Justice: Runaways, Rescuers, and Slavery on Trial* (Cambridge, MA, 2010), 205.

48. Benjamin Quarles, *Black Abolitionists* (New York, 1969), 57 and ch. 9; Kantrowitz, *More than Freedom,* chs. 5–6. Black men and women, many of them newly freed in the South but unable to remain under state laws which required them to vacate upon pain of reenslavement, created new settlements just north of the Ohio River. These became a magnet for runaways. Often the settlements were in the shadow of white Quaker towns, which celebrated them as centers of freedom and

occasionally offered protection from slavecatching raiders. Historians have seen these combinations of displaced manumittees, fugitive slaves, and black men and women attracted by the all-black settlements as islands of liberty and named them "Freedom Villages." On the use of the phrase, see Sundiata Keita Cha-Jua, *America's First Black Town: Brooklyn, Illinois, 1830–1915* (Champaign, IL, 2000), 17–18; also Heerman, "Deep River"; Cheryl J. LaRoche, *Free Black Communities and the Underground Railroad: The Geography of Resistance* (Urbana-Champaign, 2014).

49. Foner, *Gateway to Freedom,* ch. 5, esp. 134. Some 300 slaves were returned to their owners during the 1850s, most under the 1850 Fugitive Slave Act; about 3,000 escaped through New York alone. Stanley W. Campbell, *The Slave Catchers: Enforcement of the Fugitive Slave Law, 1850–1860* (Chapel Hill, NC, 1970), 199–207.

50. The following account of the confrontation at Christiana, Pennsylvania, is drawn from Slaughter, *Bloody Dawn.*

51. Campbell, *The Slave Catchers,* 117–130; Fergus M. Bordewich, *Bound for Canaan: The Underground Railroad and the War for the Soul of America* (New York, 2005), 333–339; Gary Collison, *Shadrach Minkins: From Fugitive Slave to Citizen* (Cambridge, MA, 1998); Gordon S. Barker, *The Imperfect Revolution: Anthony Burns and the Landscape of Race in Antebellum America* (Kent, OH, 2011).

52. Slaughter, *Bloody Dawn,* ch. 5.

53. Christopher Bonner, "The Price of Citizenship: African American Activism, 1827–1868" (doctoral diss., Yale University, 2014), ch. 4, p. 13.

54. Philip S. Foner and George E. Walker, eds., *Proceedings of the Black State Conventions, 1840–1865* (Philadelphia, 1979), 99–100 (Troy, NY) and 333–334 (Cincinnati, OH).

55. Jeffrey Kerr-Ritchie, "Rehearsal for War: Black Militia in the Atlantic World," *Slavery and Abolition,* 26 (2005), 1–34; and J. R. Kerr-Ritchie, *Rites of August First: Emancipation Day in the Black Atlantic World* (Baton Rouge, LA, 2007), ch. 5.

56. James M. McPherson, *Battle Cry of Freedom: The Civil War Era* (New York, 1988), 176–180; Paul Finkelman, *An Imperfect Union: Slavery, Federalism, and Comity* (Chapel Hill, NC, 1981), 282–283.

Coda: Free at Last

1. This Coda is drawn in considerable measure from *Freedom: A Documentary History of Emancipation,* especially series 1, vol. 1, *The Destruction of Slavery;* series, 1, vols. 2 and 3, *The Wartime Genesis of Free Labor;* and series 2, *The Black Military Experience.* These are a product of the collective work by the members of the Freedmen and Southern Society Project, at the University of Maryland. The Coda is part of an earlier debate on the topic "Who Freed the Slave?" See Ira Berlin, "Who Freed the Slaves?

Emancipation and Its Meaning," in David W. Blight and Brook D. Simpson, eds., *Union and Emancipation: Essays on Politics and Race in the Civil War Era* (Kent, OH, 1997), 105–122.

2. *The Statutes at Large, Treaties, and Proclamations of the United States of America,* 17 vols. (Boston, 1850–1873), 12:319.

3. Ibid., 12:376–378; 589–592; 597–600.

4. Ibid., 12:354.

5. Ibid., 12:376–378; 589–592; 597–600.

6. U.S. War Department, *The War of the Rebellion: A Compilation of the Official Records of the Union and Confederate Armies,* 128 vols. (Washington, DC, 1880–1901), ser. 2, vol. 1, 750.

7. See, for example, *Freedom,* series 3, vol. 2, doc. 7.

8. Quoted in James M. McPherson, *What They Fought For, 1861–1865* (Baton Rouge, LA, 1994), 59.

9. Ibid., 60.

10. Roy P. Basler, ed., *The Collected Works of Abraham Lincoln,* 9 vols. (New Brunswick, NJ, 1953–1955), 7: 499–502. Lincoln later said, "No human power can subdue this rebellion without using the Emancipation lever as I have done" (ibid., 7:506–508, quotation on 507).

11. Frederick Douglass, "Should the Negro Enlist in the Union Army?" speech delivered at National Hall, Philadelphia (July 6, 1863), published in *Douglass' Monthly,* August 1863.

12. John G. Sproat, "Blueprint for Radical Reconstruction," *Journal of Southern History,* 23 (1957), 25–44, quotation on 33.

13. *The Black Military Experience,* ch. 15; J. David Hacker, "A Census-Based Count of Civil War Dead," *Civil War History,* 57 (2011), 307–348.

14. U.S. War Department, Surgeon General's Office, *The Medical and Surgical History of the War of the Rebellion* (Washington, DC., 1870), part 1, vol. 1; *The Black Military Experience,* ch. 15.

Acknowledgments

Historical scholarship rests upon the work of others. *The Long Emancipation,* I am pleased to acknowledge, is an exemplar of this axiom.

First among my benefactors is Henry Louis Gates, Jr., best known to the world as "Skip." *The Long Emancipation* could not have been written without his invitation to deliver the Nathan I. Huggins Lectures at the Hutchins Center for African and African American Research, an invitation that was preceded by a semester's fellowship at the W. E. B. Du Bois Center, both at Harvard University. They were followed by Skip's invitation to transform the lectures into a book.

Following my stay in Cambridge on the Charles, I received a similar invitation from the Australian National University, where my great good friend

Douglas Craig arranged for a another fellowship that allowed me to put my ideas about abolition in front of scholars who may have known little about the abolition of slavery but, thanks to the dynamics of Australian history, knew a good deal about the intersection of race and class. My ideas were sharpened still further in discussions with Shane White and his colleagues at the University of Sydney. I left Oz far wiser than when I arrived.

Back home in the United States, I discovered that Patrick Rael, a former student at the University of Maryland, was completing his own study of the long emancipation. While my *Long Emancipation* was a slim presentation of the structure of slavery's demise, Patrick's *Eighty-Eight Years: The Long Death of Slavery in the United States, 1777 to 1865* offered a robust account of emancipation as it echoed across that Atlantic. When we swapped manuscripts, it became clear that two books that started from the same premise would be very different.

Other scholars set aside their own important work to read various versions of *The Long Emancipation,* much to my advantage. I want to thank Eric Foner, Gary Gerstle, Steven Hahn, Kate Masur, and Mike Ross for their thoughtful reviews that allowed me to expand and sharpen my argument. David Blight read the manuscript for Harvard University Press and offered a host of thoughtful comments based upon his deep understanding of antislavery as viewed through the eyes of Frederick Douglass. Kate Keane took time away from her own study of second-wave feminism, from the executive directorship of the Center for the History of the New America, and from serving as the History Department's Registrar (yes, all three!) to employ her special talent to search out typos, howlers, and other ugly formulations. Needless to say, she found all too many.

In addition to these occasional laborers, Megan Coplen, Lindy Cummings, Scott Heerman, Derek Leininger, and Amy Rutenberg served consecutive terms as graduate assistants on the long-emancipation project. In addition to hauling books from the library, laboring over a hot copying machine, and mastering the complexity of the interlibrary loan system, they spent time searching abolitionist newspapers and manuscripts, providing insights into the process of emancipation from the unique vantage point of young scholars.

When the book-length draft of *The Long Emancipation* was reduced to lecture-size bites and then expanded back into a book with all its accoutrements, two editors polished it as only masters of their craft could. I am grateful to Joyce Seltzer, who combined an editor's sensibility with a historian's appreciation for argument. She was followed by Maria Louise Ascher, whose careful line-by-line reading combined with Mr. Spock–like recognition of ill logics, improved *The Long Emancipation* in more ways than I would like to admit.

Finally, when the manuscript was complete and put into the ever-caring hands of the United States Postal Service, I recognized that the genius behind it all was my wife, Martha, who cannot be blamed for the errors in interpretation or infelicities of style, but who made it possible for me to carry this work to completion when Job-like plagues leveled our household. She is my hero.

Index